Effective Writing
Teacher's Manual and Answer Key

Effective Writing

Writing skills for
intermediate students of
American English

Teacher's Manual and Answer Key

Jean Withrow

CAMBRIDGE
UNIVERSITY PRESS

Adapted from *Writing Skills* by Norman Coe, Robin Rycroft, and Pauline Ernest (Cambridge: Cambridge University Press, 1983).

Published by the Press Syndicate of the University of Cambridge
The Pitt Building, Trumpington Street, Cambridge CB2 1RP
40 West 20th Street, New York, NY 10011-4211, USA
10 Stamford Road, Oakleigh, Victoria 3166, Australia

First published 1987
Second printing 1992

Printed in the United States of America

Library of Congress Cataloging-in-Publication Data

Withrow, Jean, 1937–
Effective writing.
Summary: A practice book for achieving writing skills
in American English in such areas as letters, stories,
reports, articles, instructions, business letters,
memos and opinion essays.
1. English language – Rhetoric.   2. English language –
Text-books for foreign speakers.   [1. English language –
Rhetoric.   2. English language – Textbooks for foreign
speakers]   I. Title.
PE1408.W6236   1987   808'.042   86-32659

ISBN 0 521 31609 X (teacher's manual : pbk.)
ISBN 0 521 31608 1 (student's bk. : pbk.)

Contents

Contents

Introduction

OBJECTIVES

Effective Writing aims to help students of American English improve their writing skills in a wide variety of texts. The various problem-solving activities included are designed to help students discover what a well-written text is and how it is different from a series of poorly connected sentences. Once students become aware of the differences, they then have the opportunity to practice skills that are needed in order to write effectively.

This book concentrates on the skills that are specific to the *writing* of English. There are other aspects of language, such as vocabulary and grammar, that are common to all uses of language. These aspects are important to writing, of course, but they are not *specific* to writing. Although the activities in this book will provide students with practice in vocabulary and grammar, this is not the main objective.

LEVEL AND PROGRESSION

Effective Writing is for intermediate and high intermediate students of American English. The book is intended for adult learners of all kinds, not specifically for one kind of learner. Thus, business students studying English can gain as much from the book as students in a college setting or those in an adult education or job-training program. In short, the skills practiced throughout the book are useful for all kinds of writing.

Effective Writing is a source book. In other words, just as the book does not teach all there is to know about writing, the material does not require students to work from the beginning of the book to the end doing all the exercises along the way. Rather, the book provides students and their teachers with material that can be exploited to suit their particular needs. For example, if punctuation is a particularly weak point for a group of learners, they can work through all the exercises on punctuation without doing the other exercises in the various chapters.

Most units can be completed in 5–7 hours of class time; the first three units will probably take less time than the later units. However, many of the activities can be assigned as homework and then checked in class, which cuts down on actual class time substantially.

STUDENTS' PROBLEMS IN WRITING

Here are some of the reasons that a student's writing may be ineffective or difficult to understand, along with the exercises that deal with that particular problem. (For a full description of these exercises, see the section "Types of Exercises" on page 4.)

a) The ideas may not be presented in an order that makes sense to a reader. See these exercises: **Organizing Ideas** and **Selecting and Ordering Information.**

b) The relation between the ideas may not be clear because of the absence, or inappropriate use, of linking words and phrases, such as *because, for example, first, on the other hand.* See **Relating Ideas: Linking Words and Phrases.**

c) The writer's attitude to what he or she is writing may not be clear: Is the writer describing, suggesting, or criticizing something? This problem is taken up in **Showing Attitude** and also to some extent in **Using Reporting Words.**

d) The ideas may not be grouped together into distinct paragraphs, or the student may begin practically every sentence on a new line. Again, the beginning of a paragraph – or the beginning of a longer text – might not start the reader in the right direction; similarly, a paragraph – or a longer text – may not end appropriately. All of these problems are dealt with in **Writing First and Last Sentences, Writing First and Last Paragraphs, Writing Paragraphs,** and, to some extent, in **Comparing Texts.**

e) A text may contain ideas that are not relevant to what the writer wants to express, or the writer may find it difficult to think of enough ideas. See **Selecting and Ordering Information** and **Adding Examples and Details.**

f) The sentences may not have clear punctuation: There may be commas and periods without any good reason, or there may be no punctuation where there should be. This is treated mainly in the **Punctuating** exercises.

While it is useful to work on all these different aspects of writing in distinct exercises, it is also important that students practice combining the separate skills in one complete, cohesive, well-written text. Opportunities for this are found in **Writing Text Based on Visual Information, Writing Text Based on a Conversation, Comparing Texts,** and **Debating Issues.** In addition, there are suggestions for further writing activities in the **Practicing Writing** section at the end of each chapter.

APPROACH

The approach is learning by doing. There are various reasons for this. First, students generally find that doing something (being active) is more interesting than being told about it (being passive). Second, if students come to understand something through learning to use their own resources to solve problems, their understanding will be more thorough, and they are more likely to retain what they have learned. Third, it is only when students put something into practice that any incorrect or imperfect learning is revealed, and it is revealed both to the students themselves and to the teacher. Experience shows that learning by doing is interesting, efficient, and, most important, successful.

Teachers should note that in some cases the stated purpose of an activity is not its only purpose. For instance, the stated objective of the **Organizing Ideas** exercises is to work out the original order of the sentences. However, in order to carry this out, students will have to concentrate on ways of joining sentences together into texts. In this case, the process of discovering words and phrases that accomplish this is in fact a more important objective than the finished product, the organized text.

GROUP WORK

Group work plays a major role in this approach. The instructions for each exercise generally suggest that the task, or at least part of it, should be done by a number of students working together in a group. This is because a group of learners will, among them, usually have the knowledge and the skills needed to do the exercises. Group size can range from two to six, but three or four is probably optimal.

An individual learner's ability to organize ideas in writing is often independent of his or her general language level. Some otherwise successful language learners may have a poor sense of organization and vice versa. However, when several students work in a group and pool their abilities, they will normally be able to contribute all the elements necessary to produce clear writing. This pooling of abilities, and the discussion that arises during the exercise, will gradually strengthen every individual's skills in writing (and, as a side benefit, in speaking) English.

Group work does not normally end with the students being given the right answer by the teacher. The students can continue to argue their way to the right answer after the small-group task is completed. For example, someone can write the various suggested answers on the board, and the class can then discuss the differences (see **Organizing Ideas**). A second way is to join each group with one or two others, and the larger groups can discuss the different solutions represented by the smaller groups. A third possibility is to split up the original groups and form others of the same size. The teacher can simply give these instructions: "Get into new groups of three or four in a way that no one else in your new group is from your old group." The students then regroup and compare solutions.

Of course, group work is not *required* for students to benefit from using this book. Teachers – and students – should feel free to be creative in the ways they approach the exercises, whether individually, in pairs, in small groups, with a teacher or tutor, or as a whole class. The possibilities are many. The book may even be used for self-study, since the Teacher's Manual contains an answer key to the exercises.

TEST PREPARATION

Effective Writing can be used to prepare students for standard writing examinations administered by colleges, universities, state and local school boards, and the like. It also provides valuable practice for the *Test of Written English*, as it includes many of the essay types used in this test as well as other standard writing tests, such as writing an essay based on a visual, comparing and contrasting, and stating an opinion.

UNITS TYPES OF EXERCISES

Units	Organizing ideas	Relating ideas: linking words and phrases	Showing attitude	Using reporting words	First/last sentences/paragraphs	Selecting and ordering information	Comparing texts	Text based on a conversation	Text based on a visual	Adding examples and details	Debating issues	Punctuating	Practicing writing
1. Formal and Informal Letters	1.1	1.2	1.3	1.4	1.5		1.6					1.7	1.8
2. Writing a Story	2.1	2.2		2.3	2.4		2.5		2.6			2.7	2.8
3. Reports	3.1	3.2		3.4	3.3	3.5	3.7	3.6	3.8			3.9	3.10
4. Articles	4.1	4.2		4.3	4.4			4.5	4.6	4.7		4.8	4.9
5. Instructions	5.1			5.2	5.3		5.4	5.6	5.5			5.7	5.8
6. Business Letters and Memos	6.1	6.2		6.3	6.4		6.5		6.6			6.7	6.8
7. Stating an Opinion I	7.1	7.2	7.3				7.4	7.5	7.6	7.7	7.8	7.9	7.10
8. Stating an Opinion II	8.1	8.2	8.3		8.4	8.5	8.6			8.7	8.8	8.9	8.10

TYPES OF EXERCISES

Each chapter contains a different combination of exercises and activities, as can be seen from the chart above. Descriptions of the different types of exercises follow and provide this information:

WHAT: A description of what each exercise type consists of.

WHY: The reason for each exercise type within the overall objective of learning to write better.

HOW: General suggestions on how each type of exercise can be approached in the classroom. More specific and detailed suggestions for each exercise are included within each chapter of the Teacher's Manual.

WHICH: A list of all the exercises of each type that are to be found in the book.

ORGANIZING IDEAS

What The sentences of a text appear in random order. Students try to recompose the text by deciding on the correct order of the sentences. Certain words and phrases have been underlined to draw attention to the part they play in joining the original text together. (Words and phrases that join sentences into unified, or cohesive, texts are called here "cohesive ties.")

There are several different kinds of cohesive ties used in these exercises. A few examples follow:

1) I worked for Union Pacific Railway. While at <u>Union Pacific</u>, I had experience in computer programming.

The words *Union Pacific* are repeated in the second sentence, and refer back to the same words in sentence 1. This repetition creates a tie, binding the two sentences together in meaning.

2) I worked for Union Pacific Railway. While <u>there</u>, I had experience in computer programming.

The word *there* in sentence 2 refers to the place mentioned in sentence 1, Union Pacific Railway. This kind of reference, a substitute word, creates a tie between the meanings of the two sentences.

3) I worked for Union Pacific Railway. <u>It</u>'s a very large company.

The word *it* in sentence 2 refers to the noun mentioned in sentence 1, Union Pacific Railway. The pronoun replaces its noun, and its use creates a tie between the two sentences.

4) My primary job was computer programming. <u>Other duties</u> included bookkeeping and filing.

Although there is no repetition of a word from the previous sentence, there is use of a synonym; *duties* in sentence 2 has a clear connection to *job* in sentence 1, and this kind of synonym reference creates a tie. Also, the word *other* in sentence 2 contrasts with *primary* in sentence 1.

These exercises require close reading on the part of students because of the need to pay attention to the underlined textual devices. The exercises give the students a good general idea of what makes a *text* different from a string of unconnected sentences. (A *text* is defined by Halliday and Hasan in *Cohesion in English* as "any passage, spoken or written, of whatever length, that does form a unified whole.")

Why

As with many classroom activities, the objective stated in the instructions – to find the right order of the sentences – is not the only purpose. In addition to providing an opportunity for group work and for class discussion, this kind of exercise helps students to see for themselves the importance of "cohesive ties" in joining sentences together into unified wholes. (Of course, these terms need not be used with students.) Moreover, by discussing the various possibilities of order for the sentences and justifying their reasons, students will gradually find out exactly how these cohesive ties operate. As pointed out earlier, students should be allowed to work out the solution on their own, and the teacher should avoid short-circuiting the discussion by too quickly telling students what the right answer is.

How

One way to do these exercises is to write or type the sentences, giving one copy to each group. The copies should be cut into strips, so that each strip has one sentence. This makes it easy for students to move the sentences around into different arrangements. Working in small groups, the students should read the texts, paying close attention to the words and phrases underlined. Each group works out the best order through discussion. When the groups have reached a conclusion, their suggested orders should be compared. The teacher, or one of the students, can (without comment at this point) write the orders suggested by the various groups on the board, producing columns that can then be compared, for example:

Group	1	2	3	4	5
	d	d	d	d	d
	f	f	f	f	f
	e	b	b	e	b
	j	e	h	j	e
	b	j	e	b	j
	h	h	j	h	h

The teacher can mark the sequences that all the groups have in common and which are in fact correct like this:

Group	1	2	3	4	5
	d	d	d	d	d
	f	f	f	f	f
	e	b	b	e	b
	j	e	h	j	e
	b	j	e	b	j
	h	h	j	h	h

The teacher can now ask the students to give their reasons for and against the sequences where there are differences. If necessary, the teacher can point out what it is in the text that gives the clue to the right order, which often means referring again to the words underlined. On the whole, the students should argue their way to the correct solution rather than simply be told what it is.

Which 1.1, 2.1, 3.1, 4.1, 5.1, 6.1, 7.1, and 8.1.

RELATING IDEAS: LINKING WORDS AND PHRASES

A *linking word* is defined for the purposes of this book as a word or phrase that shows the logical relation between sentences or between clauses.

Structurally, there are three kinds of linking words and phrases used in these exercises:

1) **Transition words** like *however, well, besides,* and *for instance:* They join two sentences together in meaning. They are generally set off by commas, no matter what position they are in, because, in a sense, they interrupt the structure of the sentence. They can begin a sentence, end it, or appear after the subject.
   Examples: I can't go. *However,* my friends can.
   I can't go. My friends can, *however.*
   I can't go. My friends, *however,* can.

2) **Conjunctions** joining two independent clauses, such as *and, so, but,* and *or:* They show a connection in meaning between the two clauses. They are generally preceded by a comma.

Examples: I want to go, *but* I can't.

This is the second invitation I received, *and* I can't accept either of them.

3) **Subordinating conjunctions** introducing a subordinate clause or phrase, such as *because, although*: The subordinating conjunction itself is part of a dependent clause and requires no commas to set it off; however, the dependent clause is followed by a comma if it begins a sentence.

Examples: I can't go *because* I'm working.

Because I'm working, I can't go.

What

In earlier exercises, the first few linking words and phrases in each passage are underlined. Students are asked to talk about what these words mean, how they link ideas, and how they are punctuated. For the rest of each passage, the linking words have been removed, and students must supply a suitable word to fill the blank, either by choosing from a given list or (in later exercises) thinking of a word themselves.

Why

Students who are learning English often have difficulty using linking words and phrases to show relationships between sentences. Correct and appropriate use of these words and phrases helps hold a piece of writing together and gives readers clues to the writer's meaning. By discussing why a certain word is appropriate in a particular context, students become aware of how these words can be used effectively and accurately. The *discussion,* or the *process* of arriving at the correct answer, is what is important. Students need to realize that there are good and bad reasons for their choices. Through doing exercises of this type, students learn to apply these same skills to their own writing.

How

Working in groups of two to four, students should first read the whole text to understand the meaning, and then discuss the underlined words and phrases in the first part of the text, answering the questions given in the instructions. This part of the activity is very important, as it prepares students for the rest of the exercise; it helps them establish criteria for the choices they will make. Students should not skip this and go on to filling in the blanks.

Groups should then select the best word or phrase to fill the blanks in the rest of the passage. The teacher should give time for consensus to be reached in each group. When each group has finished, the conclusions (and differences) can be discussed by the whole class, using a procedure similar to the one described in **Organizing Ideas,** "How." Alternatively, each group can join with one or two other groups, and these larger groups can compare their answers.

Which

1.2, 2.2, 3.2., 4.2, 6.2, 7.2, and 8.2.

SHOWING ATTITUDE

An *attitude word* can be defined as a word or phrase that shows how the writer feels about what he or she is writing. For example:

> **Obviously,** if the scandal became public knowledge, some officials would have to resign, and **personally,** I don't think that would be such a bad thing.

Here the words in bold type are attitude words.

What The attitude words have been removed from a text and students supply an appropriate word to fill the blank by choosing from a given list.

Why Words that show a writer's feeling or attitude toward a subject are especially important when a piece of writing expresses opinion, such as a personal letter, an editorial, or an argumentative essay. Such words greatly strengthen a piece of writing that intends to convince readers of something. Attitude words are not always easy to use accurately and effectively, however, as meanings are sometimes difficult to explain and differences may be subtle. For this reason, exercises such as **Showing Attitude** are useful for students. Through practice and clarifying discussion, students can gradually acquire a number of common attitude words that they can eventually use in their own writing.

How The same approach can be used for this activity as was suggested for **Relating Ideas**. Another way to follow up the small-group work is to put the passage on an overhead transparency and have individuals write their choices in the blanks. At the same time, the individual or one of his or her group members should tell why they picked each word and what attitude it shows. The class can then agree or disagree with the choices, and changes can be made until a "correct" version is accepted by all. The discussion generated by this activity is very important, since often one uses attitude words by "feel" rather than by logical explanation.

Which 1.3, 7.3, and 8.3.

USING REPORTING WORDS

What Students learn to report direct speech. The earlier units focus on common kinds of reporting words, such as *said, told,* and *asked,* and later units on less common reporting words, like *admitted, explained,* and *thought.* In each exercise, examples of several ways to report direct speech are given. Students are given practice in using a variety of reporting words, and in later exercises are asked to choose the best word to report a piece of direct speech. Often the best word also tells not just *what* a person said, but *how* the person said it. It gives a clue to the speaker's or writer's attitude. This kind of exercise should encourage students to use these kinds of words when reporting speech in their writing.

How Students can work in small groups discussing the examples of reported speech, then share their findings with the whole class. This step is vital preparation for the writing exercise that follows and should not be skipped. It is most helpful if students first talk out the sentences they will write, even if they eventually write them individually. In this way, there can be discussion of why a particular alternative was chosen or why the sentence should be in a certain tense. Volunteers can write their completed sentences on the board for whole-class discussion, or students can give their sentences to the teacher for correction.

Which 1.4, 2.3, 3.4, 5.2, and 6.3.

WRITING FIRST AND LAST SENTENCES/PARAGRAPHS

What Well-written paragraphs make a written text easier to understand. Each paragraph should usually have a first sentence that introduces or leads into the rest of the paragraph, and a final sentence that summarizes the paragraph or makes a final point or leads to the next paragraph. In an extended text (say, a report or a letter), the first paragraph should get the reader interested in the topic and, usually, should outline the main points; the last paragraph should leave the reader with a sense of completion, often by referring back to the main subject or by placing this subject in a broader context.

There are various types of exercises:
a) choosing the best answer from a list;
b) making up a suitable answer to fill a blank; and
c) writing the rest of an incomplete text.

Why Well-written paragraphs allow rapid and efficient reading of a text. It should be possible for a reader to skim through a long passage by reading the first paragraph, then the first sentence of each successive paragraph, and the final paragraph, and get an overall idea of what the text contains. The various exercises on paragraphs are meant to show students how to write first and last sentences/paragraphs that help readers easily understand the important points in a piece of writing.

Note: Of course, there are more ways of organizing paragraphs and passages than the one used here. However, native users of the language can allow themselves a wider range in their choice of expression; the learner of English, on the other hand, needs to achieve mastery of a smaller, but generally serviceable, range of possibilities.

How Again, students should work in groups when making choices; the findings of each group should be discussed by the whole class. Where writing is required, students can either work as a group, with one person functioning as the group secretary, or individually. If they work individually, it is best if they then compare and discuss their various pieces of writing in small groups before discussing them as a whole class. Several alternatives can be read aloud and/or put on the board for class discussion and critique.

Which 1.5, 2.4, 3.3, 4.3, 5.3, 6.4, and 8.4.

SELECTING AND ORDERING INFORMATION

What — Students are given the beginning of a written text, such as a letter or an article, and are asked to complete it. They are given a long list of ideas for possible inclusion. Working in groups, learners choose the most relevant ideas from the list and reject the others. The next step is to group the ideas into paragraphs, each one dealing with one aspect of the subject. Groups must also decide on the best order for the paragraphs. Finally, students should write the complete text, adding linking words, phrases, and sentences and concluding paragraphs where necessary.

Why — Students often complain about not having enough ideas on any given topic to include in their written piece. In these exercises, a list of ideas is given to the students; they then work to identify the relevant and less relevant ideas. In doing this they realize the difference between having an idea and choosing to use it. These skills can be used when students make up their own lists of ideas on a topic (for example, in the **Practicing Writing** exercises).

Of course, what one person considers relevant, another may consider irrelevant; similarly, a fact that is relevant in one circumstance may not be relevant in another. These exercises are designed to make students aware of what makes something relevant by forcing them to consider not only *what* they are writing, but also *why* they are writing and *to whom*. There is no one indisputable answer in all cases. Although some items in the lists will be quickly accepted or rejected by everybody, others will lead to disagreement. Arguments are valuable, for it is only when students are forced to defend their view that they will be able to define what relevance is.

How — Each individual should first read through the list silently, making a note of the ideas he or she would include. Then the small group should work through the list, marking off all the ideas where everyone agrees, and noting those ideas where there is disagreement. The disputed ideas should be discussed as thoroughly as time allows.

Next, individuals can silently group sentences into paragraphs, and later the group can compare individual suggestions. Individuals will then need to write out each group of sentences as a paragraph, adding the linking words, phrases, and, sometimes, sentences needed to logically connect the ideas. The final paragraph will demand the most "original" writing, as students will have to come up with their own sentences, as opposed to organizing sentences that have been supplied. A group may want to compare individuals' written paragraphs as they go along, as each person's solution will no doubt be different and students will be helped by hearing the ideas of others. There is no reason to insist that all the texts be exactly the same.

Note: Working through each step of this exercise can take up to two hours. Although this is time well spent, teachers might choose to devote less class time to this and assign some of the steps for homework.

A logical extension of this activity is to have students make up their own lists of ideas on a topic. Topics can be suggested by the class or assigned by the teacher. The class can work on their lists either individually or in groups, with a group secretary writing down all suggested ideas. Then, starting with the lists they themselves have made, groups can go through the steps outlined above. This kind of brainstorming is a valuable technique for writers, and a good skill for students to practice.

Which   3.5, 4.4, and 8.5.

COMPARING TEXTS

What   Two passages are given on the same subject. One of them is poorly written, and the other is well written. Students read the two passages and decide which one is better, and why. They are then asked either to rewrite the badly written text or write another passage based on additional information.

Why   Students can best appreciate differences between a well-written complete text and a poorly connected set of sentences by seeing the differences for themselves. The kinds of things students need to examine include organization, sentence connections, sentence variety, level of formality, degree of persuasiveness, relevance of information, style, and paragraphing. Learning to examine and identify these aspects of writing in other people's texts will help students be more skillful in critiquing and improving their own writing.

How   Working in groups of two to four, students should first read the two passages silently, and then compare their views with each other. They should ask themselves (a) which of the two is easier to follow, and (b) what are the specific differences that make one easier to understand (and hence better written) than the other. One member of the group should act as secretary, making a list of the features mentioned by the group. Then each group makes a brief report to the rest of the class. As suggested with other exercises, time should be allowed for any differences of opinion to be resolved. The teacher should try to limit his or her contributions to asking questions and guiding the discussion rather than to giving answers.

After the discussion, learners should complete the second part of the task – the writing or rewriting. If time is not available for this in class, it can be done for homework. Where possible, students should later compare their versions with each other.

Which   1.6, 2.5, 3.7, 5.4, 6.5, 7.4, and 8.6.

WRITING TEXT BASED ON A CONVERSATION OR ON VISUAL INFORMATION

What   In these exercises, learners are provided with either a conversation or visual information (a diagram, a map, a graph, or photographs). In most cases there is also a model text on a related subject. Students write a text based on the information given, using the model text as a reference.

Why   Both rewriting a conversation and writing text based on something visual require the writer to process information in a new way, first absorbing it and then transforming it by putting it into a different form. This act requires thinking and writing skills often called for in the "real world," and thus the task is a useful one for students to practice. These exercises are also included as a way of integrating all the separate skills that the other exercises treat individually. However, students do not need to have done the earlier exercises in order to tackle these.

| How | Students first look at or read silently through the given material, or they can read the conversations aloud in small groups if they wish. Then, in |

groups, they discuss which aspects of the given material can be used to carry out the task. It is suggested that students first make an outline or a list of points to include. This task can be done in groups, with discussion of what should be included in what order. The final writing task is individual, so group members should all make notes during the discussion part of the activity. Groups can then compare their ideas before students begin writing, which can be done either in class or at home.

| Which | *Writing Texts Based on a Conversation:* 3.6, 4.5, 5.6, and 7.5. *Writing Texts Based on a Visual:* 2.6, 3.8, 4.6, 5.5, 6.6, and 7.6. |

ADDING EXAMPLES AND DETAILS; DEBATING ISSUES

| What | In **Adding Examples and Details**, students are given a short text that introduces a topic and makes a few statements about the topic but does |

not give many details or examples. Students are asked to add the details and examples.

In **Debating Issues**, students read viewpoints on two sides of an issue and then write a piece explaining their own viewpoint.

| Why | Students typically have difficulty either writing anything at all about a topic or supporting what they say. These two kinds of exercise give them |

ideas for what to write and ways to support what they write. The students also practice analyzing a written piece through outlining – a skill they need when looking at their own writing.

| How | After reading through the information silently, small groups of students can discuss the writers' main points and supporting details, outlining |

these together if asked to do so. When working on the **Adding Examples and Details** type of exercise, the groups can generate a list of the details or examples that could be added to make the pieces of writing more complete. They then write their individual versions of the text. When working on **Debating Issues**, groups can talk about which speaker supports which side of the issue. Together they can list the points made on the two sides of the issue. They then write their own versions of the text individually.

| Which | *Adding Examples and Details:* 4.7, 7.7, and 8.7. *Debating Issues:* 7.8 and 8.8. |

PUNCTUATING

__*What*__   The punctuation exercises cover most uses of the main punctuation
marks (periods, commas, colons, semicolons), as well as capital letters
and apostrophes.

__*Why*__   Badly punctuated writing is usually difficult to understand and gives an
impression of sloppiness. Students can easily learn some basic
punctuation rules that help them make their writing more understandable to readers.

__*How*__   In groups of two to four, students first study models of correct
punctuation and capitalization and discuss the "rules" that underlie their
uses. Discussing why punctuation is used helps students establish the "rules" they
need to do the rest of the exercises, which they can do either individually or in small
groups. A convenient way for students to share their answers is for the teacher to put
the original text on an overhead transparency, which students then punctuate,
justifying each change as they write it. Class discussion can lead to a "correct"
version. This discussion helps students build an awareness of why they punctuate
things in certain ways, which will serve them when they punctuate their own writing.

__*Which*__   1.7 Apostrophes and capital letters
2.7 Quotation marks and commas (direct speech)
3.9 Commas in sentences
4.8 Commas, periods, semicolons in sentences
5.7 Commas and periods in a paragraph
6.7 Colons, semicolons, and commas in extended writing
7.9 Mixed punctuation (when and when not to)
8.9 Mixed punctuation (when and when not to) and paragraphing

PRACTICING WRITING

__*What*__   A variety of writing topics are given; students choose one and write, using
texts in certain parts of the chapter as models if they wish.

__*Why*__   This part of each chapter allows students more freedom than any other
exercise, asking them to integrate the various skills they have learned in
previous chapters and exercises and to practice writing complete, cohesive texts. If
they need it, they have a model to look at for help.

__*How*__   The writing assignments can either be done as homework or in class.
Either way, students may wish to discuss the topic they have chosen with
others before they begin writing as a way of clarifying and sharing their ideas.
   If the writing is done in class, students can be given 30 to 45 minutes to write, and
the teacher has a chance to hold short conferences with each student about what he or
she is doing and how. This can be an opportunity for the teacher to intervene in the
writing process, to make suggestions, to help those who get stuck, and to encourage

those who seem to be on the right track in using skills they have learned. In this initial stage of writing, attention should focus primarily on the ideas the writers are trying to express and the ways they are accomplishing the task.

After a student produces a first draft, either the teacher or, preferably, other students can read it and make suggestions about clarity of meaning and organization. This can be done in mini-conferences, in small groups, or in a quick reading and short written response by an individual. The student can then work on a second draft, making changes according to the suggestions of other readers. The revision can be done as homework or in class if there is time. The second draft can then be examined by the teacher and/or by other students, perhaps even in groups, for such things as punctuation and less important grammar points. Students should have an opportunity to work on another, final draft if they wish.

Whatever routine is followed for these writing tasks, students should be made aware that generally writing is done in stages or steps. In the first stage, writers are primarily concerned about getting their ideas on paper and do not worry about commas and spelling. The writer's task is made much easier by concentrating on one thing at a time, and students may need to be taught this. Teachers do students a disservice if they demand perfect compositions in one draft.

One way of getting the most out of this final exercise in each chapter is to have students do 10-minute writings on several of the topics suggested and one long, more carefully written, composition on one topic.

Ten-minute writings are done in the following way. Students pick one topic and free-write for 10 minutes on that topic. That is, they are asked to write whatever enters their mind during that time and to keep on writing without stopping. If they cannot think of what to write, they repeat the last idea they wrote until a new one comes along. They are not to worry about correctness, only about getting ideas on paper.

This kind of free-writing serves several purposes: 1) It allows writers to concentrate on ideas without being concerned about form. 2) It frees the hand to put on paper thoughts and ideas the writer did not know he or she had before starting to write; in other words, it is a way of exploring one's inner mind on a given topic and discovering what ideas one has and in what direction one might want to go in writing on this topic. 3) It helps the writer find out if he or she has anything to say on the topic, and if not, to reject it.

Students' 10-minute writings can be read aloud to the class as a way of sharing many different views and ideas about a given topic. Hearing others' ideas may give students additional ideas for their own writing. Ten-minute writings are generally not collected or corrected by the teacher.

Completed final drafts of longer pieces of writing on the topics in **Practicing Writing** can be shared by students in small groups or in the whole class, either by having students read them aloud or by printing them for distribution. Students then have a chance to read good pieces of writing and to discuss what makes these effective texts.

Which   All chapters include *Practicing Writing*: 1.8, 2.8, 3.10, 4.9, 5.8, 6.8, 7.10, and 8.10.

1   Formal and informal letters

Suggested procedure

Note: Throughout this Teacher's Manual, suggestions are given on how to handle each exercise with students. Please note that these are only *suggestions.* You may prefer to do things in a different way. Please feel free to be as creative as you want to!

1. Introduce help-wanted ads (want ads) in one of these ways:
   a. Ask students if they have ever answered a newspaper want ad, and if so, to tell the class about it.
   b. As a previous day's assignment, have students find want ads in English-language newspapers and then say in class what they are for.
   c. Ask students to tell what they know about want ads.
   d. Tell students what a want ad is, where they are found, and what kinds of things they advertise for.
   (Do not spend a lot of time on this portion of the lesson, as it is not the main focus. Five minutes is probably enough.)
2. Students read the want ad in the book and restate what the ad says in their own words. (You may need to tell students that *wpm* means "words per minute.")
3. Students work in groups on arranging sentences in logical order. (See general suggestions in **Organizing Ideas,** p. 5.) While students work, you can circulate from group to group. If the sentences are on strips of paper, encourage students to move the sentences around and try different arrangements. Make sure they explain why a certain order works or does not work. You will need to push students to notice the underlined words and to state the relationships or cohesive ties those words make with previous sentences. Students may need to be told why (d) is the best first sentence: It states the purpose of the letter and refers directly to the ad. When a group finishes, remind them to divide the letter into paragraphs.
4. Discuss each group's answers in the ways suggested on page 6 of the Introduction. Another variation is to have one student write out his or her group's version of the letter on the board while other groups are finishing up their sentence organizing. The whole class can then check the arrangement, show the cohesive ties with arrows (see answer below), and make changes if necessary. It is easier to see the relationship between sentences if the whole piece is written out on the board or on an overhead transparency.
5. If students do this exercise as homework, they can check their answers with others during the next class. Again, one version can be put on the board as suggested in (4).

Answer (with explanations)

Dear Ms. Cuellar:

refers to ad ↙

(d) In reference to your advertisement in the Times June 1, I would like to apply for the position of travel agent.

(g) I have an Associate of Arts degree in Travel and Tourism and have worked as an intern at Vacations Plus Travel Company. (a) My primary responsibility at Vacations Plus was helping plan international trips for individuals and groups. (e) Additional duties included typing correspondence, doing ticketing, and telephoning airlines, bus companies, and clients. (f) In dealing with clients, I was often required to use Spanish and French, both of which I speak fluently.

for the above reasons

(b) I therefore feel confident that I can make a contribution at your company. (c) I

indicates closing

enclose a resume as requested, and I look forward to hearing from you at your earliest convenience.

Paragraphing: Paragraph 1 states the purpose of the letter. Paragraph 2 gives the writer's qualifications for the job. Paragraph 3 concludes and closes the letter. Sentence (b) could also be placed as the closing sentence of paragraph 2.

1.2   *RELATING IDEAS: LINKING WORDS AND PHRASES*

In order to fill in the blanks with the best linking words and phrases, students should be encouraged to look at three things, or criteria: meaning, sentence structure, and punctuation.

Suggested procedure

1. In small groups, students discuss the underlined words in paragraph 1. Many students will want to skip this discussion and fill in the blanks immediately; you will need to push them to answer the questions asked. Each question is important in helping students prepare for the second part of the exercise.

   Discussion: (1) *Well* is an interjection that is almost a filler, similar to "You know" or "Anyway." It shows that this sentence is related in some way to the previous sentence, that it's a continuation of what the writer wanted to say in sentence 1. It is usually followed by a comma, though the comma is optional.

   (2) *But* shows contrast. The two clauses have opposite meanings in some way. When *but* connects two independent clauses, it is usually preceded by a comma.

   (3) *Besides* has the same meaning as "in addition" or "moreover" or "also." The

writer wants to add another point. When it begins a sentence, it is usually followed by a comma.

(4) *And* connects two clauses of similar or related ideas and weight. When it connects two independent clauses, it is usually preceded by a comma.

(5) *For instance* means "for example." The writer wants to cite an example. It is usually, though not necessarily, set off by commas.

2. Students continue to work in groups filling in the blanks. (See p. 7 of the Introduction.) You can go from group to group as students work, questioning their reasons for their answers. When groups are finished with blanks 6–14, they can compare answers with other groups or with the whole class. An alternative way for the class to share answers is to have students fill in the blanks on a transparency which is shown on an overhead projector. This allows everyone to see, question, and discuss what others wrote.

3. Groups do 15–18, justifying their answers in each case. After they have compared answers, an optional activity is to have students create their own sentences using a few of the linking words and phrases that appeared in this exercise. This can be done in pairs or individually, with sentences read aloud, written on the board, or handed in.

Answers

6. a) because (Both *however* and *By the way* would start a new sentence; they do not join two clauses as *because* does.)
7. a) and (This word connects a series of verb phrases – a list of things the writer does as part of his job.)
8. c) such as (The dishes listed are examples of Japanese food; *such as* introduces the list in the way the word *including* would.)
9. b) however (to show contrast with the previous sentence)
10. b) so (*Then* cannot join two independent clauses, and *because* does not make sense.)
11. c) but (to show contrast with the previous independent clause)
12. b) though (In this sentence, *though* means the same thing as *however* would; it shows contrast with the meaning of the previous sentence.)
13. b) because (the only choice that can be used to introduce a subordinate clause)
14. a) well (a filler, a loose connection to the previous sentence)
15. besides (*And* would also work, though the word *and* does not usually begin a sentence. The writer wants to add another advantage.)
16. because (the only choice that can introduce a subordinate clause; it also fits the meaning)
17. such as (introduces a list of examples); however (*However* shows contrast; *but* would work, too, but is not usually used at the beginning of a sentence. *And* would not be a good choice because it does not show the contrast in meaning between the two sentences.)
18. but (joins two independent clauses and shows contrast in meaning)

1.3   *SHOWING ATTITUDE*

Suggested procedure

1. Introduce the idea of letters to the editor in one of these ways:
   a) Ask students about letters to the editor. Where do they appear? Who writes them? Why?

b) Give an assignment the previous day: Bring in an English-language newspaper and find the Letters to the Editor page. Tell what some of the letters are about and who they are from. Summarize the main point of one letter, and tell the writer's attitude to the subject.

2. Students read the whole letter in their book silently (or aloud in small groups) to get an idea of what the writer is saying. Ask students to restate the writer's main point in their own words and to summarize his attitude toward teenagers.

3. In groups, students choose the best word to fill the blanks. You can circulate from group to group asking students to justify their answers. This task will take a lot of discussion; differences are sometimes subtle, and the exact meanings of the words are sometimes difficult. Students should be reminded to look carefully at the attitude the writer is expressing with each word he uses.

4. Groups can compare their answers with others, or new groups can be formed to share answers (see p. 3 of the Introduction). Whole-class discussion can follow, using an overhead projector to display students' answers, or by having three students write the three paragraphs of the letter on the board, or by having students read their answers aloud. There will be a lot of discussion; allow for this. It is through discussing and arguing that students will learn which word is best and why.

Answers
1. a) admittedly (The writer feels most teenagers deserve no praise, though he admits that some do.)
2. b) in my opinion (expresses his personal viewpoint)
3. b) in fact (The writer wants to emphasize the worst thing he has seen; similar in meaning to "as a matter of fact.")
4. c) clearly (meaning: it is clear; it is without a doubt)
5. a) unfortunately (The writer thinks it's unfortunate that these teenagers are not being punished.)
6. a) obviously (meaning: it is obvious; it is clear)
7. a) frankly (meaning: to be honest; admittedly)
8. c) of course (meaning: naturally; in the natural order of things)
9. b) naturally (meaning: of course; to be sure)

1.4   *USING REPORTING WORDS*

Since this is the first exercise in the book on reporting words, students simply practice the structure and punctuation changes needed to turn direct speech into reported speech. There are person changes (i.e., *I* to *he*), tense changes (i.e., present continuous to past continuous), sometimes words added (i.e., *if* when reporting a Yes-No question), quotation marks and commas deleted, and sometimes changes from *say* or *said* to *told*.

Suggested procedure

1. Students read the sample sentences of direct and reported speech either silently or to each other in small groups, or have students take turns reading them aloud to the whole class.
2. Have students describe the changes made in each sentence in reported speech, either in small groups or to the whole class. For example: In the first sentence, *I*

changes to *he, am going* changes to *was going,* the quotation marks and comma are removed, and the sentence starts with the words *Jose said* instead of ending with them. You can make note of the verb changes on the board as students talk:
 – am going → was going (present continuous → past continuous)
 – will go → would go (future *will* → past *would*)
 Paying close attention to the underlined words will help students do this.

3. Have students work in pairs or small groups, first orally telling how they will change the sentences, and then writing out the new sentences. Each student should write the sentences.

4. Students can compare their sentences in new groups. Have different students each write a sentence on the board. Mistakes should be corrected through class discussion or by other students, but not without justification and explanation by the person correcting the mistake. In this way students are building their "rules" for how to change direct into reported speech.

5. Ask students what value they can see in learning to do this kind of reporting.

> **Answers**
> 2. Fran told Sam she was going to be out of town that weekend.
> 3. Henry said he'd (he would) come.
> 4. Henry asked if there was anything Sam (he) wanted him to bring.
> 5. Sam asked him (Henry) to bring a bottle of wine. *or* Sam asked if he (Henry) would like to bring a bottle of wine.
> 6. Henry said he was sorry Fran couldn't come. (Optional: Have students try this sentence using *told*.)

1.5 WRITING FIRST AND LAST SENTENCES

Suggested procedure

1. Elicit from students what makes a good first sentence of a text. Some points to include might be:
   – There are no hard-and-fast rules; many variations are possible depending on circumstances, type of writing, style, and writer.
   – The first sentence *usually* gives the reader an overall idea of what the letter, memo, article, etc., is about (but sometimes not, depending on style).
   – *Usually,* first sentences are more general, less detailed than other sentences. First sentences may give an overview, while other sentences give details, examples, illustrations.

2. Ask students what makes a good last sentence to a text.
   – Again, there are no absolute rules.
   – The last sentence *usually* sums up what the writer said, or restates, or makes a final point – but not always.

3. Tell students to read the instructions and the letter in part A. Students, in small groups or as a whole class, orally restate to each other what the letter says. Before looking at the choices for the first sentences, they can speculate about what they think the first sentence should say. Then they should read the alternatives and discuss them in small groups. Tell students not to pick up their pens until they have decided on the best first sentence and explained their reasons to each other.

4. Students read the choices for the last sentence, discuss them, and decide on one.

Before they write, have students check their decision with others in the class or with the whole class. Be sure they give reasons for their selection.

Answers
FIRST SENTENCE: (d) It most directly states the purpose for the letter.
LAST SENTENCE: (b) It makes clear what the writer wants the Lost and Found Department to do.

5. Have students, in groups, read the letter in part B, restate what it says, and decide what its main purpose is. They should talk out possible first and last sentences before they write. Writing can be done individually or in pairs. It can also be assigned as homework.
6. Have several students put their first and last sentences on the board for discussion by the class. If the writing was done for homework, they can first compare their sentences in small groups and then pick the best ones to go on the board.

Sample answer
FIRST SENTENCE: I would like to inform you that I have found your wallet.
LAST SENTENCE: Please let me know what you would like me to do with it.

1.6   *COMPARING TEXTS: ORGANIZING*

Suggested procedure

1. Introduce the notion of letters of application for scholarships. Ask students what different kinds of information such letters should contain and in what order that information might be given. Ask what tone the letter should have; that is, would such a letter have the same tone and style as a letter to a friend or family member? What might some differences be?
2. Have students silently read both letters in part A; as they read, they should look at organization and tone. In small groups, students discuss which of the two letters is (1) better organized and (2) written in a more appropriate style. You can move from group to group to make sure students give reasons for their choices.
3. The whole class discusses which letter is best and why. Once students have agreed that the first letter is better, ask students to tell what advice they would give Rupert Bormann if he wanted to revise and improve his letter. They might suggest such things as:
   - Be more formal. Expressions like "where things are happening" and "that's all for now" sound too casual for this kind of letter.
   - Organize ideas better. Information on any given topic is scattered throughout the letter rather than gathered together into one paragraph.
   - Make your purpose for writing clear in the first sentence, not at the end.
   - Write a more appropriate ending, one that tells what you would like or expect from the person you are writing to.
4. Students now have some criteria to use when writing the letter of application suggested in part B. They may first want to discuss in small groups what information should be included and what should be left out, if any. They could also discuss what information should come first, second, and so on, and what kinds of information should be put into each paragraph. They can also discuss what the first

sentence should say. After these discussions, students should write individually, either in class or for homework.

5. Students' letters should be shared with one another. Small groups of students can read their letters to each other or can silently read each others' letters, or individuals can read to the whole class. Ask students to say what makes each letter good and give a suggestion for improvement, if they have one. An alternative would be for the teacher to collect all the letters and print the best for distribution to the class.

Sample letter

Dear Admissions Office,

I would like to apply for admission to Brooklyn Law School as a part-time student for pursuit of a degree in law starting next September. I received a B.A. degree in business from the State University of New York, Binghamton, N.Y., in June of 1985. Since then, I have been working for Legal Services in Newark, New Jersey.

My current work as a paralegal emphasizes tenants' rights and immigration law, and it is these two fields that I am interested in pursuing as a lawyer. I have also done volunteer work at St. John's Church, Hoboken, in a community legal assistance program for two years. This experience has exposed me to a variety of community legal problems and has increased my desire to receive more formal training in law in order to better help people with legal problems. I am very interested in Brooklyn Law School because of its concern for part-time students and its dedication to good legal training.

I look forward to hearing from you.

Sincerely,
Anna Peterson

Note: When you are writing a letter to someone whose name you do not know, it is often difficult to know how to address that person in the opening of the letter. The opening "Dear Sir" or "Dear Madam" used to be acceptable, but the trend today is to address the position of the person you are writing (e.g., "Dear Admissions Officer,") or the office/department that person works in (e.g., "Dear Admissions Office").

Other appropriate closings for a formal letter such as this are "Sincerely yours," and "Yours truly."

1.7   *PUNCTUATING: APOSTROPHES AND CAPITAL LETTERS*

Suggested procedure

1. Ask students to describe the reasons for each apostrophe in the sample sentences in part A. They can do this either in small groups or as a whole class. They should notice that some apostrophes show possession (e.g., *Maria's sister*) and some indicate contractions (e.g., *we'd*, meaning "we had"). Apostrophes, then, have two functions.

2. Have students work in pairs correcting the apostrophes in sentences 1–5. They can then compare their answers with another pair of students, discussing and explaining differences. The corrected sentences can be written on the board, or students can make corrections on an overhead transparency, at the same time explaining what the problems are.

Answers
1. You'll never believe whose car I rode in last week – Margaret's!
2. I'll be honest; it's not really hers.
3. It's her parents'.
4. But Margaret's learning to drive, and I'm (I am) always willing to go for a ride in a new car.
5. We're still laughing about Margaret's attempts to parallel park!

3. In small groups, students tell why capital letters are used in each set of examples in part B. Ask each group to report its findings to the class.
   (Capital letters are used for (1) titles; (2) proper names of places, such as streets, rivers, museums; (3) days of the week, months of the year, holidays; (4) nationalities, countries, and languages.)
4. Students do part C in pairs, discussing each change they make as they go along. When finished, they can compare their corrected letters with others. Finally, one student can make the changes on a transparency, or three students can write the corrected paragraphs on the board.

   An alternative is to give this part of the exercise as homework and have students compare their results the next day. In groups, they have to decide on one correct version and present it to the class.

Answer
Dear Miriam and Paul,

   Thank you for having Tony and me for the weekend. We had a great time, especially at the dinner party Saturday night. We'd never had a real Thai dinner before, and now we can't wait for our next one! Tony especially liked the frogs' legs with peanut sauce. In fact, when we got home, he went out into the yard to try to catch some frogs. He's out there every night after work. I don't know what he thinks we're going to do with them once they're caught because I'm sure not going to cook them!

   We also enjoyed the tour around town on Sunday and our visit to the Museum of Modern Art. Our walk along the river at sundown was the perfect end to a great day.

   We hope you'll come to visit us soon. There's a lot to do here, too, and we'll plan a big weekend. There's a wonderful museum with a large collection of Indian art that I'm sure you'll find interesting. Didn't you say you were free in November? Why don't you come then?

Thanks again,
Maria

5. Ask students to say what they learned about apostrophes and capitalization through these activities.

1.8   *PRACTICING WRITING LETTERS*

Suggested procedure

1. Students read through the topics silently. Remind students that this chapter has dealt with formal and informal letters. Ask students to pick out the topics that would require formal letters and those that would require informal letters. Are there any topics that could be either formal or informal, depending on who the receiver is? (h)

2. See pp. 13–14 in the Introduction to this manual for general suggestions. If students are to write a developed composition on one topic, an alternative way of proceeding is to let those students who choose the same topic sit together and talk out their letters: discuss purpose, who will get the letter, what it should contain (they can make a list of items if they wish), and what order should be followed (rearrange their lists in an appropriate order). They can suggest possible first sentences.

   Students then write individually, either in class or at home. If writing is done in class, you should circulate among the students, giving help and encouragement as needed.

3. After finishing their first drafts, students in the same groups can read their writing to each other, or have another student in the group read it silently. They can make comments on what they think is good about each letter, what needs to be clarified or better expressed, and what could be better organized. Comments can either be oral or written. Remind students that they can ignore minor grammar points, spelling, and punctuation for the moment.

   At this point, you might want to ask a couple of students who have written particularly good letters to read theirs to the class and have the class discuss what makes the letters effective.

4. Students rewrite their letters, either in class or at home, taking into consideration their peers' comments and suggestions.

5. Students either hand their letters in to the teacher or read one another's letters in small groups or pairs. This time, if ideas are organized and well-expressed, the focus can be grammar, punctuation, and spelling – in other words, editing or proofreading. Students can help one another with this task.

6. Final drafts should be shared with the class, either by having the best ones printed for everyone to read or by having some students read their letters to everyone.

7. Ask students to tell what they have learned about letter writing from the activities in this chapter and what specific skills they think they have developed.

2 Writing a story

2.1 ORGANIZING IDEAS

Suggested procedure

1. Introduce the activity by telling students that the piece they will be working on is a version of the beginning of a famous children's story. Ask students to look at the sentences silently and see if they recognize the story, and if so, to tell about it. If nobody knows the story, reassure them that it does not matter for this activity.

2. Students work in groups rearranging sentences in logical order. (See general

suggestions in **Organizing Ideas** in the Introduction, and the suggestions for 1.1.) Remind students to pay attention to the underlined words. Students may quickly notice that sentence (i) is the only sentence that mentions a person's name; thus, it is a logical first sentence.

3. When groups finish, students can compare answers either one group with another, in different groups, or as a whole class. Students should be encouraged to explain to one another why they ordered their sentences the way they did; they should be able to explain the connections between an underlined word or phrase and a previous sentence. It is best if they actually see the reorganized story on the board or on an overhead transparency so that arrows can be used to show the ties between sentences.

Answer (with explanations)

(i) Alice was beginning to get very tired of sitting in the field having nothing to do.

(d) Suddenly a white rabbit ran by her, saying to itself, "Oh dear! I shall be too late!" (b) Burning with curiosity, she jumped up to follow it. (g) The rabbit went down a hole, and she jumped in after it. (f) It was a long hole, and she fell for such a long time that she thought she might fall through to the other side of the earth. (a) Finally she reached bottom. (h) There she saw a bottle with a label that said, "DRINK ME." (c) So she did, and found that the liquid had a very pleasant flavor. (e) But as she drank, something curious happened – she began to shrink!

4. After finishing the activity, you may wish to tell students something about this story, "Alice in Wonderland." It was written by a British writer, Lewis Carroll, in 1865 as a children's story, but it appeals to readers of any age because of its satire. In the story, after falling down the rabbit hole, Alice drinks something that makes her get smaller and eats something that makes her get bigger. She finally reaches the right combination of drink and food to become the right size to get out of the place she fell into. This is only the beginning of an adventure which brings her in contact with numerous curious and interesting characters. Interested students might want to read the story, or part of it, on their own. Reading children's stories is not only a wonderful way to expand one's English, it is also a good way of better understanding a culture.

5. You may want to assign 2.8 (a) from the **Practicing Writing** section at this time. See 2.8 in this manual.

2.2   *RELATING IDEAS: LINKING WORDS AND PHRASES*

(It would be helpful to read the general introduction on **Linking Words and Phrases** in the Introduction and the suggestions for 1.2.)

For the most part, in this exercise, students will be working with linking words and phrases that show *order*. There are three kinds of order words used here: (1) those that tell points in the chronological development of a story and act as adverbs in a sentence, such as *at first, later, finally;* (2) those that indicate separate points in a list or the order of a writer's ideas, such as *first, then, finally;* and (3) those that tell the order of events of a story but are, either explicitly or implicitly, always followed by a prepositional phrase, such as *in the beginning* (of the story), *at the end* (of the book).

Suggested procedure

1. The discussion of the underlined words and phrases in part A can be done in small groups, pairs, or as a whole class. *At first* and *finally* show the order of events in this writer's story. *At last!* is used as an exclamation at the appearance of a long-awaited climax – in this case, the judges' decision.
2. In part B, small groups work out their answers, and then the groups can compare and discuss their results.

> **Answers**
> 4. b) at the beginning (The prepositional phrase *of the film* follows; none of the other choices can be followed by a prepositional phrase.)
> 5. a) at first (tells the initial event, what happens first)
> 6. b) finally (tells the final event)
> 7. c) however (shows contrast with their success in getting across the border)
> 8. c) first (tells the first item in a list of things they have to do)
> 9. b) then (tells another item in the list of things they have to do)
> 10. b) eventually (meaning: ultimately or finally)
> 11. b) at the end (A prepositional phrase follows; the other two words are not used with a prepositional phrase.)

3. As a follow-up activity, students can be asked to create their own sentences using each of the three groups of order words mentioned at the beginning of this section.

2.3   USING REPORTING WORDS

Students are given practice in using less ordinary reporting words than the ones practiced in 1.4.

Suggested procedure

1. Let students discuss the three ways of reporting the first sentence, either in groups or as a whole class. Students should be able to see that each of the reporting words gives a slightly different meaning: *Admitted* implies that Eva knew she had made a mistake, was willing to own up to it, and perhaps was a little ashamed of it; *thought* implies that Eva was not completely sure she had made a mistake; *announced* implies that Eva was sure she had made a mistake and was willing to tell someone all about it. Students should also notice the verb tense change and the optional use of the word *that*.
2. Students work in pairs or small groups changing the sentences to reported speech first orally and then in writing. Each student should write the sentences.
3. Students can compare their answers with each other. (See suggestions for 1.4.)

Answers
1. Eva thought (that) she had made a big mistake.
2. She explained (that) she had just typed 11 pages of her story on the computer and it had disappeared.   or   She explained that the 11 pages of her story she had just typed on the computer had disappeared.
3. She admitted (that) she had forgotten to press the save key because she was so involved in her story.
4. She doubted (that) there was any way to get it back again.
5. She insisted (that), no matter what people say, computers are not more efficient than typewriters.
   (*Note:* It seems more natural here not to change tenses, as she is making a general statement about computers and what people say about them.)
6. She suggested (that) when people write on a computer, they (should) press the save key often.

2.4   WRITING FIRST AND LAST SENTENCES

Suggested procedure

(See suggestions for 1.5.)
1. Have students read the story in part A either silently or aloud in their groups. They can then orally retell the story to one another. Encourage students to speculate about what the first sentence could say before looking at the choices and choosing the best sentence.
2. Groups discuss what the last sentence could say and then choose the best last sentence.
3. Groups compare their answers, justifying their decisions.

Answers
FIRST SENTENCE: (b) This choice is the best "lead" into the story. The other choices are either too general, such as (c), or have very little to do with the specific story told.
LAST SENTENCE: (d) This sentence seems a good summing up of the point the storyteller wanted to make. Choices (a) and (b) seem irrelevant to the story, and (c) is a little too serious for the humor of the story.

4. Students read the first and last sentences given in part B and share ideas on who the people might be and what could have happened to make their time enjoyable. They can then write individually, either in class or for homework, or in small groups.

The answer is at the teacher's discretion. Any reasonable story should be accepted, as long as the story makes a logical connection between the first and last sentences.

Sample answer
But the best thing about the vacation was the people we met by accident on the beach the first morning we were there. They were a group of "senior citizens" on a tour sponsored by a natural history museum, and their curiosity about our surroundings got us totally involved in finding out as much as we could about the flora and fauna on that beach. We weren't members of their group, of course, but they made us feel that way. In fact, by the second day, we were joining their walking tours and relaxing with them over a glass of iced tea. I think they really

appreciated having a few younger people with them, especially the children. We spent one evening singing and telling ghost stories and another evening dancing. It turned out that the age difference made very little difference. Our interests were similar, and that was all that mattered. That should give you some idea why we had such a good time together.

5. Students will enjoy sharing their stories with one another, as a great deal of variety is inevitable.

2.5   COMPARING TEXTS: SENTENCE CONNECTIONS

(See the Introduction for general suggestions.)

Suggested procedure

1. After students understand the task, they can read the two versions of the story aloud in their groups (or in the whole class). Hearing the stories aloud will help them decide which version of the story is written in a more interesting way.
2. Groups can compare their decisions. When explaining their choice, students should point to particular differences (for example, the use of the word *unfortunately* in story B, and the use of connecting words like *after*, *when*, and *so* in story B, compared to very simple, almost boring, sentences in story A.)

> **Answer**
> Story B is better. The lead sentence of story B identifies the main character by using the words "a man," whereas story A refers to the person as "He." Also the sentences of story B are well joined together, and this makes it easier for the reader to follow and more interesting to read. There is more variety in sentence types used in story B than in story A.

3. Ask students to write a paragraph telling the story of someone in their family. It may help students to tell someone else the story before writing it. They should then write the story quickly, concentrating on getting the ideas and events down on paper. They may then want to read it aloud to someone to make sure the story is clear. Then, when rewriting the story in final form, they can focus on varying the linking words and sentence types. This final writing can be done for homework, or students can help one another in class.

2.6   WRITING TEXT BASED ON A VISUAL

1. In groups, students choose six photos and decide what order to put them in to make a story. They can invent any details they need to relate the photographs and create an interesting story. After talking out the story in the group, individuals write the story.
2. Students share their stories in their group by reading them aloud. Members of the group should be encouraged to tell each reader what works in each person's story and what could be changed to make a better story.

3. Individuals revise their stories based on feedback from their group.
4. Revised stories can be read in small groups, shared with the whole class, or handed in. Alternatively, new groups can be formed, and students can read their stories to their new group.
5. If you wish, students can work in pairs on editing their stories before handing them in.

2.7   *PUNCTUATING: QUOTATION MARKS*

Suggested procedure

1. Students discuss the differences in punctuation and capitalization in each pair of sentences given as examples in part A. They should notice that end punctuation precedes a quotation mark, and that commas are usually used to set off a quotation from the rest of the sentence. The word that begins a quotation is always capitalized unless it is a continuation of the sentence being quoted (example 4c). You may wish to point out that this story is a *fable* (a brief narrative that makes a point or teaches something; a fable often uses animals as characters).
2. In part B, students may find it easiest to "hear" where the quotation marks go by reading the sentences aloud. Their punctuated sentences can be put on the board or on an overhead transparency.

Answers
5. "Where are you going?" asked the rabbit.
6. "I," announced the dog loudly, "am going to hunt rabbits."
7. "That's very nice," the rabbit said quietly. "Where will you find them?"
8. The dog replied knowingly, "There are dozens of them near the brook."
9. "Well," the rabbit mumbled, "good luck in your hunting."
10. "Just a minute!" shouted the dog. "You look like you know something about rabbits."
11. "Yes, I do," the rabbit said in a soft voice.
12. "Tell me what you know!" the dog roared.
13. "I know enough," whispered the rabbit as she hopped off into the bushes, "to recognize a good escape when I see one."

3. An optional additional activity could be to have students write down a brief conversation using direct speech to make sure they know how to use the punctuation marks. Students can then be asked to say what they learned about punctuating quotations through these activities.

2.8   *PRACTICING WRITING STORIES*

Instead of waiting until students have worked through this entire chapter (or most of it), you may wish to assign these topics as students have finished each activity in the chapter. For example, after students have completed exercise 2.1, they could then write topic (a) of 2.8; and so on. Of course, you can also do this activity last, having students write on the topic or topics that interest them, using the other exercises as models if they wish.

Suggested procedure

(See Introduction for general suggestions and 1.8 for additional suggestions.)
1. Whatever topic students write on, you may wish to give them an opportunity to talk out their stories first, as mentioned in 1.8.
2. If possible, students should also be given a chance to write several drafts, with an opportunity for readers' feedback between the drafts; this is discussed in more detail in 1.8.
3. When students have shared their compositions with one another, they can be asked to tell what they have learned about writing stories from the activities in this chapter and what specific skills they think they have developed.

3   Reports

3.1   *ORGANIZING IDEAS*

Suggested procedure

1. Introduce the activity by asking students what they know about newspaper reports. What kind of information does a newspaper report give? Where is the most important information in such a report? What questions should be answered in a newspaper report? Students should be aware that a newspaper report is factual; it does not give opinions. The most essential information is generally at the beginning of the report. Good newspaper reporters learn to give information that answers the questions who, what, where, when, and how (and sometimes why) when they write their news reports.
2. Students work in groups rearranging sentences in logical order. (See general suggestions in **Organizing Ideas** in the Introduction and the suggestions for 1.1.) Remind students to pay attention to the underlined words. Students will notice that sentence (g) tells the most essential information in this report, and therefore is a logical first sentence.
3. Students should divide the report into three or four paragraphs. The answer below gives the report as four paragraphs: the first identifying what happened to whom, the second telling about the damage, the third telling how it happened as reported by witnesses, and the fourth describing what would be done about it. The first two paragraphs could also be written as one paragraph, however, making the report three paragraphs instead of four.

Answer

(g) Yesterday evening two boats collided in thick fog in the Pacific Ocean not far from Prince Rupert, British Columbia. (c) One was a cargo ship carrying lumber, apparently on its way to Prince Rupert. (i) The other was a Canadian National ferry on its regular run from Vancouver to Prince Rupert.

(e) Fortunately, there were no casualties among the crews or passengers, but both ships suffered damage close to the water line. (a) In spite of this damage, the two ships managed to reach Prince Rupert under their own steam.

(f) According to eyewitnesses, neither of the vessels was going very fast at the time of the accident. (b) However, because of the weather conditions, the captains did not realize the danger until a few seconds before the collision took place. (h) Consequently, there was insufficient time for them to prevent the accident.

(j) A spokesman for the port authorities said that a committee would be set up to determine the cause of the collision. (d) The official added that government experts would be invited to join the committee.

4. In comparing their answers, students may reason that paragraph 3 (as above) could go before paragraph 2. However, the information in paragraph 2 (about casualties and damage) is probably more essential to readers than the information in paragraph 3 (about what caused the accident), and therefore should be given first. It is good to let students discuss their answers at some length, as it is through saying their reasons for what they do that they – and students around them – learn about such things as logical order, sentence connections, and paragraphing.

3.2 RELATING IDEAS: LINKING WORDS AND PHRASES

(You may wish to read the general introduction on **Linking Words and Phrases** in the Introduction and in 1.2.)

Suggested procedure

1. The discussion of the underlined words and phrases can be done in small groups, pairs, or as a whole class. Encourage students to read the *whole* report before beginning to work.

(1) *For the most part* means the same thing as "in general" or "generally." It is usually set off by commas.

(2) *For example* means the same as "for instance" and is usually set off by commas. This sentence gives a specific example of the courteous staff.

(3) *Even though* means "although"; it shows a contrast. (The same meaning could be expressed with *but*: I was not identified as an inspector, but a very polite porter was right there to take my luggage and escort me to my room.) *Even though* is a subordinating conjunction.

(4) *In addition* means "besides" or "moreover." It signals that the writer wants to add a point. It is a transition phrase that usually demands commas.

2. Small groups work out their answers for the rest of the exercise, and then groups can compare and discuss their results.

Answers

5. a) however (It shows a contrast between the good things found and the few things that need to be improved.)
6. a) first (This item is the first in a list of three things the writer describes as problems.)
7. b) in fact (This is the only phrase listed that works with this punctuation, sentence structure, and meaning. It means "as a matter of fact." The writer wants to mention another problem, inadequate elevator service, to explain the first problem, slow elevators.)
8. b) second (The second problem as seen by the inspector; the second item in his/her list.)
9. c) when (The only word that fits the meaning intended.)
10. b) however (to show contrast with the previous idea)
11. b) so (to show a result of the fact that tools were needed)
12. a) finally (the writer's final point or item in the list of problems)
13. d) as well as (The writer wants to give two reasons of equal importance.)
14. a) or (connects two items of equal importance in a negative statement)
15. b) on the contrary (meaning: just the opposite is true)
16. c) on the whole (meaning: for the most part; in general. It is usually set off by commas.)

3. As a follow-up activity, students can be asked to create their own sentences using the words that show a writer's order of ideas (*first, second, third, finally*).

3.3 WRITING FIRST PARAGRAPHS

Suggested procedure

1. After reading the instructions for part A, have students read through the report and then, before reading the choices given, suggest what information the first paragraph should or could contain. They should understand that the first paragraph has to identify what the report is about.
2. Students make their choice for the first paragraph and share their answers and reasons with other groups.

Answer

FIRST PARAGRAPH: (c) Paragraph (a) introduces the concern of the report (the question of hours), but only in a vague way. Also, the style is too informal for a report to a company president. Paragraph (b) is appropriate in style, but it does not introduce the report; it gives irrelevant information in discussing other aspects of the same problem. Paragraph (c) is the most appropriate because it introduces the content of the report (the feasibility of allowing workers to use flex-time), and it is in a style appropriate to the report as a whole.

3. After reading the report in Part B, students work on writing a first paragraph. They can write as a group, with one person acting as secretary, or they can discuss the contents of the first paragraph in groups and then write individually either in class or at home. When finished, they should compare their paragraphs. Some paragraphs can be put on the board, or the teacher can collect them and read or publish the best ones for discussion.

Sample answer

This report concerns the feasibility of shortening the school semester to 10 weeks. The most important concern is, of course, that each class should still total the same number of hours as in a 12-week semester. The suggestion of a shortened semester was made to the Dean of Students by a group of students and teachers.

(Any answer that accurately tells what the report contains should be accepted as long as the style is appropriate.)

3.4 USING REPORTING WORDS

As in 2.3, students are given practice in using less ordinary reporting words than the ones practiced in 1.4. Most of the reporting words used in this exercise can be followed by the word *to* (e.g., *promised to, offered to, intended to*).

Suggested procedure

1. Let students discuss the two ways of reporting the example sentence. They should see that the word *offered* allows the writer to use fewer words to tell what the contractor said and in addition indicates *how* he said it. Students should also notice what words were left out by using *offered to paint* instead of *said he would paint*.
2. After discussing sentence 1, students work in small groups or pairs changing sentences 2–5 to reported speech first orally and then in writing. Each student should write the sentences.
3. Students can compare their answers. (See suggestions in 1.4.)

Answers
2. The contractor offered to throw in the paint at wholesale prices.
3. He intended to finish the job by Friday if nothing went wrong.   *or*   He intends to finish the job by Friday if nothing goes wrong.
4. The contractor asked to finish it up on Saturday if he couldn't do it by Friday.   *or*   The contractor asked if he could finish it up on Saturday if he couldn't do it by Friday.
5. He boasted (that) he had never had a dissatisfied customer yet.

3.5   *SELECTING AND ORDERING INFORMATION*

(You may wish to read general information about this type of exercise on p. 10 of the Introduction.)

Suggested procedure

1. Introduce the topic in one of these ways:
   a) Write the word *overpopulation* on the board and have students suggest words they associate with this one. As they give words, you write them on the board in any arrangement around the topic word. After 15–20 words appear on the board, have the students who suggested each word explain how the word relates to the topic. (For example, if the associative word was *problem*, the student might say: "Overpopulation is a problem in many countries today.") Students can then choose any three words and explain how those three ideas are related. (For example, if the student picks the words *birth control, hunger,* and *problem*, the relationship might be explained in this way: "In some countries, birth control is encouraged to combat the problem of hunger.")
   b) Elicit from students what they know about the problem of overpopulation and what is being done about it in various countries in the world.
2. After telling students that the topic of this report is overpopulation, ask students to read the instructions for this exercise. Have one student restate what the instructions say.
3. Have students read the title of the report and the first paragraph. Have someone restate what the paragraph says. Ask students to predict what the rest of the report might say.
4. Students can now read through the sentences given under "Other points to consider." As they read, they should put a check mark in front of points they consider important to include in this report.
5. In groups, students discuss which points to delete and which to keep. Not everyone in each group needs to agree on exactly the same items, but students should be able to explain why they want to delete or include certain points.
6. After making decisions about relevant points, students should discuss how to group the sentences into paragraphs. Again, there may be more than one way to group the points.
7. Individuals write out the body of the report, adding linking words and phrases (and perhaps sentences) where needed. If class time is inadequate, the writing can be done for homework and brought to the next class for discussion.
8. After sharing one another's writing, students can discuss what, if anything, should be added in a conclusion. They can then write their conclusions individually.
9. Final reports should be shared with the whole class. Students will want to see the various ways of "solving this problem," as there are many variations possible.

Sample answer (with added words and sentences underlined)

[First paragraph]

    India's population will be near one billion by the year 2001; population growth is high, at 2.3 percent. <u>Consequently,</u> the Indian government encourages families to have only two children. However, family planning in India at present is voluntary, and because many Indian parents think that two sons and one daughter is the ideal small family, families are often larger than two children. In fact, the average family today has 4.3 children.

The Chinese government has imposed a policy of one child per family, but, because sons represent security in old age to Chinese parents, it is not easy for China to administer this program. China tries to enforce its one-child policy with strong peer pressure, financial rewards for having only one child, and financial penalties for having more than one child.

Kenya is one of seven African countries that have the world's highest population growth rate, at 4.1 percent. Thus, Kenyan government officials encourage people to have fewer children and to use family planning. However, for many people in Kenya, family planning clinics are far from their homes, and for religious reasons and because of custom, many Kenyans oppose birth control. Also, in Africa, having many children is traditionally considered a gift, and having none, a great curse.

It is true that government leaders in many countries are trying to do something about the problem of overpopulation in their countries by encouraging smaller families. However, their efforts are not always successful because of people's traditional beliefs and practices. Thus, the problem of overpopulation continues to be a serious one. It will probably take more than family planning clinics and financial rewards for people to change their ways.

3.6   *WRITING TEXT BASED ON A CONVERSATION*

(You may wish to read general information on this type of exercise on p. 11 of the Introduction.)

Suggested procedure

1. After reading the instructions, students should read the conversation, preferably aloud. They can do this in small groups, pairs, or in the whole class. Have one or two students restate what the important points of the conversation were.
2. In groups, students make a list of the points they want to include in a letter reporting the burglary. All students should make notes. Each student then writes a letter. Remind students to divide the letter into paragraphs.
3. Students share their letters with one another and, if you wish, with the whole class. Students may want to give one another feedback on their letters in small groups, discussing such things as whether or not the important points were included and the tone (level of formality) of the letters. If students have the time, they may wish

to rewrite their letters incorporating other students' suggestions. This could be done for homework. Students will realize that many versions of this letter are possible.

Sample letter

Dear Anna and Pierre,

I hope you're both well and enjoying North Carolina. Unfortunately, I've got some very bad news for you. Your apartment was burglarized. I can assure you that I was being careful, and that I had locked all the doors and windows. I'm very sorry about the whole thing. Let me tell you what happened.

Last Thursday night I came back from my computer class just after 11:00, and I found the whole place a big mess. The burglar (or burglars) had forced the lock on the door, and then they went right through the apartment, turning everything upside down. It was a real mess, but now I've more or less put things back in their places.

They took the radio, stereo, television set, and some paintings. I'm afraid I can't tell you exactly what they took out of the drawers because I don't really know what was in all of them. This is a problem because the police insist on having a list of the missing items before they start their investigation. I know it would be a great inconvenience, but if one of you could come back, it would be a great help. I'm very sorry for the trouble.

Hope to hear from you soon.

Your friend,
Julie Stein

4. *Note:* Other possible closings are "Fondly," "Affectionately," "Yours," and "As always."

3.7   *COMPARING TEXTS*

Suggested procedure

(See suggestions in 1.6.)

1. Introduce the notion of letters of recommendation. Elicit from students the purpose of such letters and what information they contain. Students should be aware that people applying for jobs ask former employers or colleagues to write letters of reference that highlight their strengths and give a prospective employer information about the candidate.

2. Have students silently read the two letters in part A. As they read, they should pay attention to relevance of information and sentence variety. In small groups, students discuss which letter is better written.

3. The whole class discusses the two letters. Students should be able to come up with some of the following reasons for choosing letter 1.

Answer

Letter 1 is better than letter 2. Version 2 contains some personal information and views which are not appropriate for a formal recommendation such as this. In addition, there are a few phrases which use a style that is too informal for this kind of report. Finally, the sentences are more varied and interesting in version 1 than those in version 2.

4. Students may wish to discuss in small groups what points should be included in the letter about George Isher in part B. They could also talk about what should come first, second, and so on. Students then write individually, either in class or for homework.
5. Students share their letters.

Sample letter:

I have been asked to write a letter of recommendation for Mr. George Isher. I am very pleased to do so. I have known Mr. Isher since working with him in 1981 when he worked as an intern in our company.

Mr. Isher is a pleasant, easy-going person, one who likes people and who is equally liked by people. He is very honest and responsible. In addition, he is a person who does a job carefully and thoroughly.

Mr. Isher is skilled in computer programming; he knows programming well and has taught several courses on the use of computers. He is also a good organizer, which is evident from the complicated computer systems he sets up. Mr. Isher is bilingual in Russian and English, and he reads Spanish. He also types 80 words per minute accurately.

I recommend Mr. Isher highly for a job requiring the kinds of skills he has.

6. You might ask students to summarize the characteristics of a good letter of recommendation.

3.8 WRITING TEXT BASED ON VISUAL INFORMATION

Suggested procedure

1. Students read the report in part A about drilling conditions and relate it to the diagram. It is not absolutely necessary for students to know the exact meanings of all words; for *basalt*, for instance, they only need to know that it is a certain kind of rock. If you wish, you can ask students to restate in their own words the essence of the report.
2. In part B, students work in groups preparing a report based on the map given. They should first talk about the road conditions orally, describing each piece of the road to each other. This will help prepare them for the writing. They may need help with some of the vocabulary. After their discussion, they can write the report individually or in pairs.
3. Students read their reports to one another. They should discuss whether or not each report is true to the diagram. They may also want to talk about such things as paragraphing and verb tense.

Sample report

The road from Bellevue to North Bend is fairly level. At North Bend, it rises sharply from sea level to an elevation of 6,270 feet at the Snoqualmie Summit. As we left North Bend and started climbing, the road became curvy, especially as we went through the forested area just outside of North Bend. It straightened out the higher we got, though.

After you leave Snoqualmie Summit, the road drops down to an elevation of 3,010 feet at Lake Easton. Just after Lake Easton, as the road passes a dam, there are very sharp curves. This lasts for a short while. Then the road passes through two tunnels before you get to Cle Elum.

Up until this point, the road was paved. However, it became unpaved outside of Cle Elum, and eventually we were forced to take a detour. This detour was not only unpaved; it was extremely rough. This lasted until we got to Thorp.

All of this time, the road gradually descended until it finally reached an elevation of 607 feet at Ellensburg. The first half of the stretch between Thorp and Ellensburg was unpaved and very rough. However, about halfway, we again hit paved road. For this last part of the trip, the road conditions were good.

Note: Both present and past tense were used in this report, past to refer to the trip that was taken, and present when referring to road conditions that were presumably unchanged at the time of this writing.

3.9   *PUNCTUATING: COMMAS*

Most of the common uses of commas are exemplified in this exercise. You can reassure students that if they know how to use commas in these instances, they will understand the most important uses of commas in English.

Suggested procedure

1. Introduce the concept of a book report. (A book report or review gives an idea of what the book is about and discusses the reviewer's reactions to it.) Ask students where they might find such reports and if they have ever written one.
2. Have students read through the entire book report (parts A and B), either silently or aloud to each other. Have students restate the plot of *Foreigner* and the writer's reaction to the book.
3. Students discuss, in small groups, the reasons for each comma in sentences 1–6.
4. Students share their findings. They should come up with the following comma "rules":
   (1) Use commas to set off unnecessary information inserted into a sentence.
   (2) Use a comma between two independent clauses joined by a coordinating conjunction.
   (3) Use a comma to set off a transition word or phrase.
   (4) Use commas to set off relative clauses that are unnecessary to the meaning of the sentence.
   (5) Use commas to separate items in a list of three or more. (In this case, the items are noun phrases.)
   (6) Use a comma after a dependent clause when the dependent clause begins the sentence.
   (7) Use a comma before a quotation.
   Of course, students do not have to use these grammatical terms to describe the use of commas. Any language will do, as long as they get the idea across.
5. Students work in pairs or small groups punctuating sentences 7–15 in part B.
6. Groups compare their results. An overhead transparency or the blackboard is a good way to do this. Encourage students to refer back to the sample sentences to "prove" their use of each comma.
7. As a follow-up activity, students could write six of their own sentences showing these six different uses of commas.

Answers

7. Although Feri never completely and finally answers these questions for herself or the reader, the novel ends with a resolution that at least for the moment satisfies the reader.
8. I recommend this novel highly, not just because it deals with an experience common to many people who have adopted a new country, but also because Ms. Rachlin has succeeded so well in making Feri's experiences and feelings real to us.
9. In fact, once I started reading the book, I couldn't put it down.
10. For one thing, Ms. Rachlin's ability to make every incident, even the smallest, contribute to the feeling of tension and conflict compelled me to read on to the end.
11. In addition, her expertise in describing the sights, smells, sounds, and tastes of Iran helped make me feel exactly what Feri felt.
12. Because I was very involved in her story, I wanted to know how it came out.
13. The fact that there were questions unanswered at the end of the novel may make some readers uncomfortable, but I didn't feel that way.
14. I liked making my own guesses and creating my own fantasies about Feri's future.
15. In short, I loved *Foreigner.*

3.10 PRACTICING WRITING REPORTS

Suggested procedure

(See the Introduction for general suggestions and 1.8 for additional suggestions.)
1. Students can either choose one topic to write on in depth, or they can write on several of the topics as 10-minute writings. (See Introduction.)
2. Students may wish to talk out their reports to other students in small groups, as mentioned in 1.8.
3. If possible, students should be given a chance to write several drafts, getting feedback from others on each one. This is discussed in more detail in 1.8. Some of the writing can be done for homework and some in class.
4. Students should share their completed compositions with one another.
5. Ask students to say what they learned about report writing through the activities in this chapter.

4 Articles

4.1   *ORGANIZING IDEAS*

Suggested procedure

1. Introduce the activity by putting the word *archeology* on the board. Ask students to tell what they know about archeology and what archeologists do. *(Archeology* is the study of the evidence remaining from people's life and culture of past ages; archeologists are the people who are specialists in this science.) Ask students if they know of any archeological sites (places where archeologists are digging to find artifacts from the past), or if they know of the Mayan Indians (a race of Indians in southern Mexico and Central America whose civilization reached its height around A.D. 1000). The article they will read is about scientists discovering an ancient Mayan tomb. Students may need help with some vocabulary:

    > *tomb:* a vault or room serving as a burial place for a dead person
    > *skeleton:* the bones of a person or animal
    > *inscriptions:* writings or engravings on stone, wood, paper, or other surface
    > *coffin:* a container in which a dead person is buried
    > *looters:* robbers
    > *pictographs:* pictures representing words or ideas
    > *hieroglyphics:* a system of writing with pictures

2. Students work in groups arranging the sentences in logical order. Students may notice that sentence (b) identifies where and when the tomb was discovered, and therefore is the best first sentence.
3. When groups finish, they can compare their results. The rearranged sentences should be put on the board or on a transparency and the connections between sentences explained by students. Students should also explain where they started each paragraph and why. They will probably notice that paragraph 1 is about the newly discovered tomb at Rio Azul, paragraph 2 is about the tomb at Palenque, and paragraph 3 talks of both tombs.

Answer

(b) In the thickly grown remote jungles of northern Guatemala at Rio Azul in May of 1984, archeologists located an ancient painted Mayan tomb. (g) The tomb was thought to be more than 1,500 years old and, much to the satisfaction of the archeologists, had never been touched by looters. (e) Included in the contents of the newly discovered 1,500-year-old tomb were elaborate wall paintings, pottery, and a male skeleton. (a) Scientists hoped that the last item, the male skeleton, would help them determine whose tomb it was and how Mayans of that era lived.

(d) Archeologists explained that a great deal was learned about the Mayans from another similar tomb, found in 1952 in Palenque, Mexico, which also contained a skeleton, that of Pacal. (f) By deciphering the inscriptions on Pacal's stone coffin, or sarcophagus, archeologists figured out that this ruler was born in the year 603 and died in 683. (h) In addition to the sarcophagus inscriptions, these archeologists used pictographs found in the tomb of Pacal to help them understand Mayan hieroglyphics and Mayan history.

(c) In short, archeologists hope that the new tomb at Rio Azul will be as fruitful and significant for the study of the Mayans as Pacal's tomb at Palenque.

4.2   *RELATING IDEAS: LINKING WORDS AND PHRASES*

1. Introduce the article by asking students what they know about nuclear power. Put the word *hazard* on the board and elicit a definition from students. (A hazard is a risk, a danger, or a peril.) Ask students to read the title of this article and to predict what the article will be about. If students suggest some hazards, list them on the board.
2. Students should read the article silently; then ask one student to tell the class what the article says. Compare the students' list of hazards on the board with the ones mentioned in the article.
3. Have students read the instructions and then discuss in groups the underlined words 1–4 in paragraph 1. (1) *First* is used to show the writer's first item in a list of hazards. (2) *Although* means the same thing as "even though" and shows contrast. (3) *Namely* means the same thing as "that is"; the writer wants to specify exactly

what two methods of transport are meant. A comma is optional after *namely*.
(4) *Since* means "because" in this sentence.

4. Students, in groups, choose the best words for numbers 5–13. Then they should compare and explain their choices to one another.

Answers
5. a) second (the writer's second point)
6. b) so (meaning: consequently; as a result)
7. b) for example (The writer wants to give examples of where the wastes can be stored.)
8. c) however (To show contrast with the previous statements. *By the way* is possible grammatically, but makes the idea expressed in the sentence too unimportant.)
9. b) since (meaning: because)
10. a) third (The writer's third point. Students may be tempted to choose *In conclusion.* This is not an appropriate choice since this paragraph is not a conclusion to what the writer is saying; it contains the writer's third point.)
11. a) so (coordinating conjunction meaning "therefore")
12. b) nevertheless (It means "however"; shows contrast.)
13. b) though (It means "however"; it never appears at the beginning of a sentence, only in the middle or at the end.)

4.3 WRITING FIRST AND LAST PARAGRAPHS

Suggested procedure

1. After reading the instructions, have students read the body of the article about Mrs. Gordon. Then, before looking at the choices for the first paragraph, have students suggest what information the first paragraph should contain.

2. Students, in groups, discuss the choices for the first paragraph and pick one. They can then share their decision and reasons with other groups.

Answer
FIRST PARAGRAPH: (b). The first two sentences of choice (a) would be suitable, but a third sentence is needed that properly leads into the article about Mrs. Gordon and the traffic offenders she deals with. Instead, the third sentence, though it mentions Mrs. Gordon, talks about traffic laws in general, not this specific one. Choice (c) does not identify Mrs. Gordon and what she does. Choice (b) identifies Mrs. Gordon and tells what she does. In addition, the last sentence leads into the rest of the article. For these reasons, (b) is the best first paragraph.

3. Students can suggest what the last paragraph should contain before reading the choices. Then, in groups, they read the choices and select the best one. Again, they should share their findings.

Answer:
LAST PARAGRAPH: (c). Choice (a) contains some irrelevant details. Also, the use of the first person ("I") is inappropriate in a news article, and the end of the paragraph is more appropriate for a persuasive essay than for a newspaper article. Choice (b) is an inappropriate ending for this article because it focuses on money, which the article did not mention at all. Choice (c) seems the best choice. It describes Mrs. Gordon's attitude to this kind of offender and restates her reasons for doing what she's doing.

4.4   *SELECTING AND ORDERING INFORMATION*

Suggested procedure

1. Introduce the topic in one of these ways:
   a) Write the words *shopping by computer* on the board and have students suggest words they associate with this phrase. As they give words, write them on the board in any arrangement around the topic phrase. After 15–20 words appear on the board, have the students explain how each word relates to the topic. (For example, if the associative word was *catalog,* a student might say, "Shopping by computer is similar to using a catalog to shop through the mail.") Students can then choose any three words and show how they are related. (For example, the relationship of the words *expensive, fun,* and *catalog* might be explained this way: "Shopping by computer is probably more *expensive* than shopping by *catalog,* but it's more *fun.*")
   b) Ask students what they know, if anything, about shopping by computer. If they know little, ask them to speculate about how it works and what the advantages and disadvantages might be.
2. Students read the title and the first paragraph and restate in their own words what the paragraph says. Have students predict what the rest of the article might say.
3. Students read through the sentences under "Select from these points." As they read, they mark the points they consider important to include in this article.
4. In groups, students discuss which points could be included and which are not relevant. They do not need to be in total agreement on this.
5. Having picked certain points to include, students group them into possible paragraphs. You may need to encourage them to explain what relationships they see and why they want to group certain points together. Again, they may not agree totally on the groups, but the discussion should help them clarify what they want to say and in what order they want to say it.
6. Individuals, or pairs, write out the body of the article, adding necessary linking words and phrases (and, perhaps, sentences). Writing can be done in class or for homework.
7. Students share their results and determine whether their articles need conclusions. If so, they can discuss what their conclusions should say and then write them. They can read one another's articles and perhaps choose the most successful ones to be read to the whole class. There will be many different ways of completing the article, depending on what the writer decides to emphasize.

Sample answer (underlined words are added)

[First paragraph]

Teleshopping is convenient for people, especially those who don't live near large cities. For one thing, you can buy the same items at home as you can in stores. There's also the matter of time. One user says, "I can shop by computer at midnight if I want to without worrying about stores being closed."

Convenience is not the only advantage to teleshopping. One user reports that it is much more fun than going out to shop. In addition, prices for items bought through a computer can be lower than store prices because of lower overhead costs.

Some people, however, see definite drawbacks to teleshopping. These people feel that computer shopping is nothing more than a new video game, and an expensive one at that. In most cases, in fact, there is a charge for belonging to such a teleshopping service, for example, $25 per year. Also, it is still very difficult or impossible to put a picture of an item on a computer screen. In fact, the easiest items to sell through computer today are such things as tickets and well-known appliances that do not need salespeople and pictures.

However, the teleshopping business is still young. Although only a small number of households own a computer today, there are at least five such teleshopping services in operation right now, and many more are predicted in the years to come. Despite the disadvantages people see in teleshopping, it will probably be a big business in the future.

8. Ask students to say what tasks this activity required and to tell how these same tasks could be used when writing a composition of their own. Students should understand that they could pick any topic, brainstorm a list of ideas similar to the list of points they saw in this exercise, and then select points from that list to organize into a composition. It is one approach to writing a composition.

4.5   *WRITING AN ARTICLE BASED ON A CONVERSATION*

Suggested procedure

1. After reading the instructions, students should read the conversation, preferably aloud. They can do this in small groups, pairs, or as a whole class. Have one or two students restate some of the important points made in the conversation.
2. Students read the outline begun at the end of the conversation. In groups, they should complete the outline, adding other points of difference between the two cultures mentioned in the conversation. Other points they might add include:
   - United States: husband home at dinnertime
   3. Work
      - Japan: workers often stay with same company for life; often discuss personal problems with boss
      - United States: workers often change companies; make direct demands for raises or promotion; keep photos of family on desks
3. After completing the outline, students can write their compositions using the outline as a guide. They may want to discuss with one another such things as interesting ways to begin the article, paragraphing, what examples to include, and how to end the article. Remind students of where the article is to appear and who will read it.
4. Students share their articles with one another. They may want to give one another

feedback and, if there is time, revise their articles. Students will realize that many versions of this article are possible.

Sample article

Japanese who work for a few years in the United States find that there are some differences between the culture of their home country and that of the United States. These differences in social life, family life, and work life can cause some surprises for the Japanese businessperson.

A Japanese businessman is accustomed to socializing with his colleagues on weekends, especially for such activities as playing golf. However, weekend socializing with one's colleagues does not happen very often in the United States, though occasionally colleagues will get together for such things as a barbecue. When that happens, however, the whole family is invited, which is not the case in Japan. Also, people in the United States usually dress much less formally than Japanese do for such functions. In fact, Mr. Kawashima, one of our employees who just returned to Japan from two years working as a manager in the United States, reports that he was quite embarrassed the first time he was invited to his boss's home for a barbecue, as he was the only guest to appear in business clothes. Other guests wore jeans or shorts.

Family life is different, too. In Japan, the husband often works late and then has a drink with his colleagues, whereas in the United States, the husband is usually home earlier for dinner if at all possible.

As for the work situation, people in the United States seem to take more initiative for their careers than they do in Japan. That is, people in the United States are direct in asking for a raise or a promotion, and if they do not get what they want from their company, they readily switch to another company. Thus, few people continue to work for the same company for their whole work lives. Just the opposite is true in Japan. People generally stay with the same company all of their lives. One other difference in work life that Mr. Kawashima reported was that it is not very usual for American workers to talk over personal problems with their bosses, while in Japan this is a frequent occurrence.

Working and living in another country can make a person aware of many interesting and sometimes surprising differences between the cultures of the two countries. At least, this is certainly true of Japan and the United States.

4.6 WRITING AN ARTICLE BASED ON VISUAL INFORMATION

Suggested procedure

1. Introduce the topic in part A by asking students if they know the term *UFO* (unidentified flying object) and what they know about UFOs. They should understand that some people believe they see objects flying in the air and sometimes landing which they insist are from outer space (e.g., other planets, or other solar systems). Scientists are not certain whether these objects exist or not. This article seems to show that the sightings of UFOs are affected by what people see and read in the media, thus implying that UFOs do not exist, or at least not in the numbers people think.

2. Students read the instructions and work in groups, reading the article and underlining parts of the article that refer to different parts of the graph. The first paragraph of the article is given here with underlining to show how students can do this.

During the early part of January of this year the rate of UFO reports was steady, around three or four per week. When, however, on Monday, January 16, a science fiction film about visitors from outer space was shown on television, there was an immediate sharp increase in reports of sightings from all parts of the state. The commanding officer of Tawukee Air Force Base, General Wayne Tyler, who is directly responsible for the investigation of all such reports, decided to make his findings known. On Monday, January 30, the Iowa *Chronicle* carried an article written by Tyler, which maintained that all UFO reports could be explained quite naturally by civil and military aircraft movements. Following this explanation, there was a rapid drop in the number of reported sightings, although the rate remained above the prebroadcast level.

3. In groups, students work on the task in part B, writing an article about immigration to the United States from 1820 to 1980. Before writing, they should look at the graph and make statements about it orally to make sure they understand the information on it. For example: "From 1920 through 1960, most of the immigrants were Europeans. After that, the largest numbers were from the Western Hemisphere." (*Western Hemisphere* refers to immigrants from South America, Central America, the Caribbean, Canada, and Mexico.) Then they should read the facts accompanying the chart and relate them to each 20-year period on the graph, thus noticing possible causes for increases and decreases in the numbers of immigrants in various categories. It will help students if they talk out the relationships of the facts to the graph before they begin writing.

4. Students then write their articles, either in pairs or individually. Since there is a lot of information given here, two or three students could decide to divide up the material and each write about a different time frame. When they finish writing, students should read one another's articles, checking for accuracy of information. If necessary, revisions can be made.

5. Students share their articles with the class or with other groups. Students will see that there are many ways to write an article on this topic. Because there is so much information given, different students will decide to include and leave out different things, depending on what they want to emphasize or what they think is important. There is no one right way to do it.

6. You may also want to ask students what value they see in doing this kind of task. They may need to be reminded that many jobs require this type of writing, based on a graph or visual figure of some kind.

Sample article

Throughout the history of the United States, the number of immigrants to the United States and where these immigrants came from have been greatly affected by events both inside and outside the United States. For example, in the period from 1820 to 1840, there was a slow, steady increase in the numbers of people immigrating to the United States from Europe largely because of the doubling of the European population and the rise in unemployment due to the Industrial Revolution. The Irish potato famine from 1845 to 1849 made that number even larger, especially as ocean travel became safer.

From 1860 to 1880, there was a slight increase in the number of Chinese immigrants because these people helped to build the railroads in the West.

However, in 1882, the Chinese Exclusion Act limited Chinese immigration, so the numbers of Asian immigrants again went down, while the numbers of Eastern Europeans and Italians increased.

The year 1907 showed the highest number of immigrants admitted to the United States: 1,300,000. While the greatest numbers were still Europeans, 85%, there was an increase in the percentage of immigrants from the Western Hemisphere, from 5% in the previous 20-year period (1880–1900) to 10% in this 20-year period (1900–1920). Immigration decreased somewhat after 1907 because the 1917 Immigration Act excluded Asians and required immigrants to be literate. The numbers continued to decrease from 1920 to 1940 because of the Stock Market Crash and Great Depression within the country from 1929 to 1935 and because in 1924 immigrant quotas were established for each country outside the Western Hemisphere. During this period, 60% of the immigrants came from Europe and 36% from the Western Hemisphere.

Starting in 1948, war refugees were admitted to the United States, so the numbers of immigrants gradually increased between then and 1960. The period from 1960 to 1980 saw large percentages of immigrants from the Western Hemisphere and Asia, 46% and 31%, while the numbers from Europe decreased to 22%. During this time various refugee acts allowed refugees to be admitted to the United States, and in 1965 the Immigration Act opened more immigration from the Third World. In 1980 the number of immigrants admitted was about 500,000, quite a drop compared to the number admitted in the year of greatest immigration, 1907. Though the numbers have been steadily increasing since 1940, one wonders if they will ever reach the peak of 1907.

4.7   ADDING EXAMPLES AND DETAILS

(You may wish to read information about this type of exercise on p. 12 of the Introduction.)

Suggested procedure

1. Introduce the topic by asking students to speculate about what the term *communicative styles* means. Reassure them that they will find out more after reading the first paragraph of this article.
2. Students read the instructions. One student should restate what the tasks are. Then students read the first paragraph. Ask them what they have found out about the title of the article.
3. Students read the rest of the article, noticing the blanks which they will fill in with information, and then read the chart at the end. In groups, students should discuss what they could add to each paragraph using the chart for additional information. Students may need help with vocabulary in the article and in the chart. In fact, this might be a good opportunity for students to first do some vocabulary work, working in small groups to pool their knowledge and using dictionaries where necessary for words that are new to some of them. Before using dictionaries, however, students should be encouraged to guess word meanings from the context. For example, for the term *systematic inquiry* students know already that this person is objective and likes logic and ideas. They can almost guess from the word *system* that *systematic* means orderly, so a Thinker likes to study things in an orderly, organized way.

Some Definitions (in the order the words appear):
clash: to conflict or disagree
personality clash: people who don't get along because they have two different
    kinds of personality
objective: not influenced by emotion or personal prejudice (opposite: subjective)
perceptive: have ability to perceive; the quality of being understanding, sensitive
wordy: talkative
impersonal (in speech): not personal, without emotion
unpredictable (in clothing): cannot be predicted or known in advance; unexpected
specific (in speech): definite; explicit
abrupt (in speech): short; curt; not talkative

4. When students complete their compositions, they can share them with other
   groups.

Sample of expanded composition:
   [First paragraph]
   The *Intuitor* is an "idea" person, a problem solver, a person who likes theories
   and looks to the future. The speech of intuitors is often wordy and impersonal, and
   their writing tends to sound intellectual. Intuitors wear clothing that is mixed in
   style, often unpredictable. They are most likely to be lawyers, engineers, scientists,
   or accountants.
   The *Thinker* is objective; he or she likes logic, ideas, and systematic inquiry.
   Thinkers are businesslike and specific in speech and well-organized in their
   writing. They dress conservatively, and are most likely to be scientists and
   researchers.
   The *Feeler* is warm, perceptive, and personable; he or she works well with
   human emotions. Feelers' speech is friendly and humorous, while their writing
   tends to be personal. In dress, they are informal and colorful. They are likely to be
   entertainers, teachers, or nurses.
   The *Sensor* is a doer, one who emphasizes action and getting things done.
   When they talk, sensors are abrupt and direct, and their writing is similarly brief.
   Their clothing is informal and simple. Sensors most likely choose to be executives,
   salespeople, or managers.
   [Last paragraph]

4.8   *PUNCTUATING: COMMAS, PERIODS, AND SEMICOLONS*

(You may wish to read 3.9 for common uses of the comma.)

Suggested procedure

1. Introduce the topic, supermarkets, by asking students to look at the illustration of
   a modern supermarket and compare it with a small grocery store or small specialty
   stores, such as butcher shops and fruit markets. You may want students to read the
   whole article at this point to understand the content.
2. Make sure students know the words for these punctuation symbols:
   . (period)
   , (comma)
   ; (semicolon)

Have students discuss the first three sentences in small groups, comparing the three ways of writing the same information. Sentence 2 uses a comma rather than a period or a semicolon because the coordinating conjunction *but* joins the two independent clauses. Sentences 1 and 3, however, have no coordinating conjunction. Therefore, a symbol is needed to show the end of a sentence. A semicolon can replace a period when the ideas in the two sentences being joined are closely related. Semicolons can also be used when two related sentences are linked together with a transition word or phrase. For example:

Many people find large supermarkets convenient places for buying their groceries; however, others prefer the intimacy of small grocery stores.

3. After discussing the three sentences as a whole class, students continue in their groups to correct sentences 4–9. They then compare their results as a whole class by writing the sentences on the board or correcting the sentences on an overhead transparency. There will be different ways to correct the sentences, as students have the option of adding connecting words if they wish.

Answers (with added words underlined and alternative punctuation marks in parentheses)

4. The modern supermarket is very different from the small grocery store of yesterday; (.) it's bigger, and it offers a greater variety of services.

5. Shoppers in today's supermarkets don't have a lot of time to spend shopping, (.) so they look for convenience and efficiency.

6. Managers of supermarkets cater to this. (;) They offer many convenience foods, but they try not to sacrifice freshness or quality.

7. Managers also recognize their customers' desire for relaxation. (;) They pipe in calming music, and they use soft colors for decorating.

8. You can do many things besides shop for food in today's supermarket. (;) You can purchase prescriptions from the pharmacy section, (.) you can get your hair cut at the beauty shop, (.) or (and) you might do your banking in the banking area.

9. Today's shoppers enjoy the convenience of modern supermarkets, but (; however) they also miss the uniqueness of small grocery stores.

(There are other ways to punctuate these sentences. Students may choose to use transition words like *however* or *therefore* instead of conjunctions like *but* and *and,* for example, and this is fine as long as they use a semicolon or a period before these transition words. You will have to use your discretion in accepting their changes, since not all possible answers are given.)

4.9   *PRACTICING WRITING ARTICLES*

Suggested procedure

1. To help students pick one topic to write on, you might give groups time to "buzz" about each topic; that is, students read each topic out loud and talk a minute or two, saying whatever comes to their minds about the topic. Once they have chosen a topic to write on, students can talk in more detail about their topic, either in their own small group or in a group of students all writing on the same topic.

2. The topics in this chapter may take a little research. One way to proceed is to let students first free-write for 10 minutes about their topic (see Introduction). They can then share what they have written with others, understanding that the writing was done only to start thinking about the topic. Students can then be encouraged to write down a number of questions they need to find answers to before writing more on the topic. Their homework assignment for the next class could be to read something about the topic or to talk to knowledgeable people about it in order to find answers to some of their questions. (Keep in mind, of course, that students are not writing research papers!) Armed with more information and perhaps using some of their ideas from their free-writing, students can then begin to write their first draft, either in class or at home.

3. Students share their first drafts with one another, getting questions and suggestions about focus, content, organization, and clarity from other students. They can then write second drafts, perhaps for homework, and then work together, if time permits, on editing their articles. Final copies should be shared with the class.

4. You may wish to have students tell what they have learned about writing in general and about writing articles in particular from the activities in this chapter.

5   Instructions

5.1   *ORGANIZING IDEAS*

Suggested procedure

1. Introduce the topic by asking students to look at the illustration and define in their own words each of the computer parts. If students do not know the computer parts, reassure them that they will know more about how computers work after doing this exercise. Remind them that this chapter deals with instructions; this activity tells how to insert a disk and prepare a computer for operating. Students may need help with some vocabulary:

display screen: monitor; the TV-like screen on which words and graphics appear
power light: light that tells when the power is on
keyboard: typewriter-like keys through which you give instructions to the computer
disk: flat plastic piece that contains information for computer to read; tells computer what to do
disk drive: machine that reads a disk

2. Students work in groups arranging sentences. When they finish, they compare their answers with other groups, explaining why they put the sentences in the order they did. They should notice the ties between sentences, perhaps marking them with arrows. Caution students who are familiar with computers that all computers are different; they should pay attention to the underlined clues when making decisions rather than relying on their knowledge of how their computer works.

Answer

(d) To start with, turn on the display screen (monitor). (a) Next, push up the switch on the back of the computer to turn on the computer. The POWER light on the keyboard will light up in a few seconds. (c) After the POWER light comes on, press the RESET key in the upper right corner of the keyboard. (g) After pressing the RESET key, wait until the red light on the disk drive goes off, and then open the disk drive door. (f) Once the disk drive door is open, the disk drive is ready to receive the operating disk. (h) Now, remove the disk from its envelope, hold the disk with the label up, and gently slip the disk into the disk drive. (b) Once the disk is in, close the disk drive door. (e) Finally, press the RETURN key; after a few seconds, a message on the display screen will indicate that the computer is ready to operate.

indicates order

5.2 USING REPORTING WORDS

Suggested procedure

1. Students read the example and discuss the two ways of reporting the quotation. They should discover that some reporting words, in this case *warns* (or *warned*), allow one to change the wording of what someone said without changing the meaning and, at the same time, show how Luigi said it. They will notice, also, that the reporting verbs are in present tense in this exercise. This is acceptable, since this advice is something Luigi always tells tourists, not something he told them once in the past. Of course, past tense would be acceptable, too.

2. Students read number 1 and then work in pairs or small groups on numbers 2–6. They can make the changes orally first, then in writing.
3. Students compare answers.

Answers

2. He explains that if drivers know pedestrians see them, they'll just blow their horns and race through the intersection.   *or*   He explains about drivers blowing their horns and racing through the intersection if they know pedestrians see them.
3. Luigi encourages people to look for others who want to cross the street at the same time, since there's safety in numbers.   *or*   Luigi encourages people to cross the street with others (at the same time as others), since there's safety in numbers.
4. He reminds people to be careful even with a green light because cars don't always stop for a red light.
5. Luigi begs people not to ever hold their hand(s) up like traffic police trying to stop cars. That technique is for the inexperienced.
6. Luigi urges people to take a deep breath, say a prayer, and walk across resolutely with eyes straight ahead.

4. Students, individually or in pairs, write their own examples of reporting sentences using some of the reporting words given in the exercise. An alternative activity would be for students to create an exercise for other students similar to this one: Write short pieces of direct speech with three choices of reporting words for other students to change into reported speech.

5.3   WRITING PARAGRAPHS

This exercise gives students practice in writing a short, logically ordered paragraph giving instructions on how to do a simple task.

Suggested procedure

1. Students read the instructions and the sample paragraph in part A. In small groups or pairs, they circle the words that tell *order*. They should circle:

First,   Next,   when,   Before,   If,   Now,
Meanwhile,   Finally,   when,   If,   If

They may notice that some of the words are *transition words* (*first, next,* and so on) and some are *subordinating conjunctions*. Of course, the terminology is not important; only the usage is.
2. Students read the instructions for the task in part B and the situations described. After choosing a situation, students should be encouraged to make a list of the steps needed for their situation and then to talk through their instructions with a partner before writing. Then they can write their paragraphs.
3. Students ask someone to read their paragraph to check clarity. They can then work on revising their paragraph and making sure they have used some *order* words. The revision could be done for homework. You will want to encourage them to include a diagram if it would help clarify their instructions.
4. Students share their final piece with the class.

5.4	**COMPARING TEXTS: ORGANIZATION**

Suggested procedure

1. Students read instructions to part A and talk in groups about what changes were made in the revised letter and why they were made. The revised letter has better paragraphing (each paragraph is devoted to one specific task) and better order (the first task described is the first one Maria is to do in the morning), and is better written (unnecessary information is removed and one sentence, the last, is rewritten). The result is a tighter, more readable letter.
2. In small groups, students read the instructions to part B. They read the letter and discuss what can be done to improve it. Remind students what was done in part A: reordering, reparagraphing, rewriting, and deleting information. Encourage students to outline or list the main points before writing.
3. Each student writes the revised letter. This could be done as homework.
4. Students share their letters.

Sample revision:
Dear Lillian and George,

We're happy that you're going to be subletting our apartment for the month of July. Anita has told us a lot about you, so we feel we almost know you. As requested, here are a few instructions.

You can pick up the keys from our downstairs neighbor, Jan, but call her first to make sure she'll be in (665–3031). There are five keys, three for the apartment door and two for the main door. Please return the keys to Jan when you leave.

One responsibility you'll have is taking the mail out of the mailbox every day. The mailbox key is hanging on a nail on the back of the door.

Another thing we ask is that you water the plants every four or five days. Please don't forget those on the porch. They'll need water almost every day unless it rains. Of course, feel free to use the terrace for sitting, sunbathing, or whatever. Just be sure to lock the porch door when you finish.

Use any of the kitchen utensils and bedding you want. The bedding and towels are on a shelf in the bathroom.

If there are any phone calls for us, you can tell people that we'll be back August 1. Our number is 218–936–1127. Our landlord can be reached at 536–1819 if you have trouble with plumbing, refrigerator, or electricity. If you need help with anything else, you can always ask Jan, or Ron, who lives next door. That's about everything, I think. Enjoy your stay!

Sincerely,
Henry Knorr

5.5	**WRITING TEXT BASED ON VISUAL INFORMATION**

Suggested procedure

1. Students work in pairs. One student can read the instructions in part A; the other can point out the route on the map. The reader should check what the listener is doing to make sure instructions are followed correctly.
2. Students work in pairs on part B. They first list places for the visitor to see; then

they write the directions, using the given instructions as a model of how to write them. Encourage students to include at least five stops.

3. Students give their written instructions to other pairs of students to see if the directions are accurate. They can revise them, if necessary.

4. You may want to ask students to read their instructions aloud to the whole class. They should notice that there are many different ways of completing the task.

5.6 WRITING TEXT BASED ON A CONVERSATION

Suggested procedure

1. Students read the conversation, preferably aloud, in pairs, small groups, or as a whole class. Have students restate some of the main points made.

2. In groups, students list the important points in the order they wish to report them.

3. Individual students (or pairs) write out the instructions. When finished, they can share their writing in their groups and then with the class.

Sample outline of important points

1) make sure you want to do it
2) research the field, gather information
   - talk to experts
   - read
   - check out competition
   - do market research: need, customers, desired services, competition
3) plan
   - get experts for board of directors
   - budget
4) hire good people
   - listen to them
   - encourage their professional development
5) get more training
   - classes
   - consultants for seminars, problem solving

Sample instructions

How to Start Your Own Business

First make sure you really want to start your own business, because it takes a lot of time. Once you are determined to do it, you need to research the field. This includes making sure no one else is doing exactly the same thing in your area. Find out how much need there is for your kind of service, locate the customers, and find out what kind of services they want. You'll want to talk to experts, potential customers, and potential suppliers, and you'll want to do a lot of reading.

Then you need to plan. Make sure you have experts on your board of directors. Make up careful budgets and plan for everything, even the number of paper clips.

An essential is hiring smart people. You can learn a great deal from them. You should also encourage them to continue to grow professionally by letting them attend seminars and development courses.

Pay attention to your own training too. Take courses in business administration, if possible. It's not only a good way to learn, it's also a good way to make contacts. People you meet in your courses could become your consultants. At times you will want to hire consultants to help you solve problems or to give you and your staff seminars on particular issues.

Just remember, getting started in a business takes a lot of time and energy. You may spend a whole year on research and planning before you actually open your business, but it pays off in the end.

5.7   *PUNCTUATING: COMMAS AND PERIODS*

Suggested procedure

1. Students, in small groups, discuss the use of commas in part A. Students should notice that commas could not be used in place of periods because then sentences would run together. They may need to be told the meaning of the abbreviations:

   c. = cup   tsp. = teaspoon   T. = tablespoon

   Reasons for commas
   Once the water is boiling again,: Dependent clause at the beginning of a sentence.
   Let the rice cook, without stirring, / Add the butter and parsley, without stirring,:
     Extra information inserted into a sentence.
   After 5 minutes,: Dependent clause at the beginning of a sentence.
   uncover the pan, toss rice with a fork . . . parsley, and serve . . . : Words in a list
     (verb phrases).

2. Students write out the paragraph in part B, adding commas, periods, and capital letters. When they have finished, they compare their results with others in their group. The group should agree on one correct version to present to the class.

   Answer
   SPANISH-STYLE CHICKEN

1 chicken cut into pieces	1 tsp. finely minced garlic
½ tsp. salt	1½ c. chopped green or
¼ tsp. black pepper	red peppers
1 T. butter	⅓ c. dry white wine or water
1 T. oil	2 c. diced tomatoes
½ c. chopped onion	1 bay leaf

   Salt and pepper the chicken pieces and set them aside. Heat oil and butter in a large heavy skillet. Add chicken, putting skin-side down, and cook over medium-high heat 5 minutes. Turn and continue cooking about 5 minutes, turning occasionally. When chicken pieces are brown, add onion, garlic, peppers, and wine or water. Cook about 10 minutes, stirring, and then add tomatoes and bay leaf. Cover and let cook 20 minutes. Uncover and cook 10 minutes longer.

5.8   *PRACTICING WRITING INSTRUCTIONS*

Suggested procedure

1. Once students have chosen a topic, encourage them to make a list of the steps needed to do the task. With this list, they should orally give the instructions to someone else to make sure the steps are in order and are complete. If necessary, they can revise their lists based on their partner's feedback.

2. Students write out their set of instructions in paragraph form (or several paragraphs, if needed.) Some instructions need a diagram or map. Encourage students to use *order* words as in 5.3 if appropriate.

3 Students read their writing to others in their group for comments and suggestions and revise if needed. They should share their final drafts with others in the class.

6   Business letters and memos

Even if your students are not in business, they can benefit from the exercises in this chapter. For one thing, everyone has to write a business letter at some time. For another thing, the writing skills practiced here are general; they apply as well to academic and other kinds of writing. Of course, students who are in business will appreciate the chapter, especially for the *form* of business letters and memos.

6.1   ORGANIZING IDEAS

Suggested procedure

1. Introduce the exercise by asking students what topics they think a business memorandum, or memo, can cover. They should understand that a memo can be about anything a person in a company wants to communicate to others in the same organization, including an announcement such as this one.
2. Ask students to read over the sentences and tell the subject of this memo (an announcement of someone's death).
3. Students work in groups arranging the sentences in logical order. Encourage students to look for and explain to each other the relationships between the underlined phrases and previous sentences. (Students may be unfamiliar with the word *condolences*, meaning an expression of sympathy with a person in grief.)
4. Groups compare their results when finished. The rearranged sentences should be put on the board or on a transparency and the connections between sentences shown with arrows and explained by students. Students should also explain where they started each paragraph and why.

Answer

(g) It is with deep regret that I announce the death of our office manager, Ms. Margaret Len. (d) As many of you know, she had been ill for some time, and on Tuesday underwent emergency surgery. (c) Unfortunately, this was unsuccessful, and she died in her sleep the next day.

(e) Only a few days before this, she had been in contact with office personnel by phone, still very concerned about the new health benefit plan that she initiated last year. (i) The health plan was a typical product of Ms. Len's interest in employees' well-being, and it made her much appreciated by all employees. (b) She was equally appreciated by people outside the company for her active participation in community groups, especially the Public Library Volunteers and Literacy Volunteers. (h) Within the firm, on the other hand, she will be best remembered for her loyalty to, and her concern for, all members of the staff. (f) Anyone with a personal family problem, for example, could always count on her sympathy and support.

(all of the above) ⬅ (a) I am sure, therefore, that all of you will join with me in sending condolences to her husband and family.

Note: This way of paragraphing makes paragraph 1 about the death, paragraph 2 about Ms. Len's contributions to the company and others, and paragraph 3, the writer's invitation or suggestion that everyone send condolences. Students might also suggest making sentences (h) and (f) part of paragraph 3, so that paragraph 3 concerns the company. This would also be acceptable.

6.2   *RELATING IDEAS: LINKING WORDS AND PHRASES*

Suggested procedure

1. Students read the whole memo and restate the writer's main points.
2. Students read the instructions and then discuss the meaning and punctuation of the underlined words in paragraph 1. (1) *First* shows the writer's first suggestion; it is followed by a comma because it's a transition word at the beginning of the sentence. (2) *Since* means "because" in this sentence. (3) *In contrast* means the

same thing as "on the other hand" or "contrary to this"; it is set off from the sentence with a comma. (4) *Therefore* means "thus" or "for these reasons"; it is followed by a comma, as it is a transition word.

3. Students, in groups, choose the best words for numbers 5–12. Then they compare and explain their choices to each other.

Answers
5. a) second (the writer's second point)
6. b) for instance (The writer wants to give an example of when they will need computer programming services.)
7. a) however (to show contrast between having their own computer programmer and hiring one part-time)
8. a) third (the writer's third point)
9. c) thus (meaning:therefore)
10. a) although (meaning:even though)
11. c) moreover (adding another point or argument to the one already given)
12. c) in addition (adding another point besides the argument about saving money)

4. *Optional:* Students can choose some of the linking words and phrases used in the memo and write sentences of their own showing their use. This could be done as homework.

6.3   *USING REPORTING WORDS*

Suggested procedure

1. Students read the example and discuss the two ways of reporting the quotation. They should discover that some reporting words, in this case *admitted* and *promised*, allow one to change the wording of what someone said without changing the meaning. Fewer words are needed than when *said* is the reporting word.
2. Students read number 1 and then work in pairs or small groups on numbers 2–5. They can make the changes orally first, then in writing.

Answers
2. The accountant thought (that) what those people said about overcharging was complete nonsense and suggested (that) they compare their prices with those of some of their competitors.
3. The foreman insisted (that) there was something wrong with those machines and warned about injury if people used the machines before they were properly serviced.
4. The director's assistant reminded Mr. Johnson that the area was a private one and threatened to call security if he didn't leave the (that) office at once.
   or The director's assistant reminded Mr. Johnson about that area being a private one . . .
5. The director promised Mr. Fong not to tell anyone what he said and urged him to put his comments on paper for the record. *or* The director promised Mr. Fong that he wouldn't tell anyone what he said and urged him to put his comments on paper for the record.

Note: The sentences above are given as one sentence. Students could divide them into two sentences if they wish. As should be obvious, there is more than one way to do this task.

3. Students, individually or in pairs, write their own examples of reporting sentences using some of the reporting words from the exercise. They should read the example before starting.

6.4   WRITING FIRST AND LAST PARAGRAPHS

Suggested procedure

1. Students read the first three paragraphs of the memo in part A, restate what it says in their own words, and suggest the contents of the fourth (last) paragraph.
2. In groups, students read and discuss the choices given for paragraph 4. After picking one, they should explain their decision and reasons to other groups.

> **Answer**
> LAST PARAGRAPH: (b). Choice (a) adds another problem (other people had larger stands) and points out the effect of these problems; however, it doesn't suggest a solution. Choice (c) is somewhat positive about the company's sales and talks of thinking about the future, but again does not suggest a solution. Choice (b) makes concrete suggestions and asks for others' reactions. It seems the best way to end this memo.

3. In groups, students read the letter in part B. They should restate the contents of the letter and suggest to one another what should be included in the first paragraph. They then (individually or in pairs) write the first paragraph. The writing could be done for homework.
4. Students compare their first paragraphs.

> **Sample first paragraph**
> Dear Mr. Duval:
> We have received your letter acknowledging our order #13492 for calculators and typewriters. However, there are several problems which we feel need to be clarified before we can give you the go-ahead on the order.

6.5   COMPARING TEXTS

Suggested procedure

1. Students discuss the two help-wanted ads, stating what qualifications are required for the two jobs.
2. Have students silently read the two letters, paying attention to organization, tone, and relevance of information. In small groups, students discuss which is the better letter and why.
3. The whole class discusses the letters. Students should be able to come up with some of the following reasons for choosing letter 1:

> **Answer**
> Letter 1, for the following reasons:
> 1) Letter 1 organizes ideas into paragraphs, whereas letter 2 has no paragraphs and scatters information all over in no order at all.

2) The purpose for the letter is clear in the first sentence of letter 1; this is not the case in letter 2.
3) Letter 2 contains information in the last sentence that is probably unnecessary.
4) Letter 2 has no appropriate ending; letter 1 ends with information about the applicant's availability for an interview.
5) Letter 1 has a more formal and pleasing tone; letter 2 sounds a bit informal and "pushy," for example: "I think I am the right person for the job," and "I think you should consider my application seriously."

4. Students work in pairs rewriting letter 2, keeping in mind the above points. Before writing, they should list in order the points they want to make, marking where paragraphs will begin. They should also decide how to begin and end the letter. Then they can write individually (for homework or in class) or in pairs.
5. Students share their completed letters.

Sample letter
Dear Mr. Terry:
   I am writing in response to your advertisement in the *Honolulu Star Bulletin* of July 1, 1990, for the position of Production Manager.
   I have worked for the Topp Clothing Company since 1979, and since 1982, I have been Assistant Production Manager. This position has given me a great deal of experience in supervising from 15 to 20 people in the production of both cotton and synthetic clothing.
   I earned a degree in Textiles from Manoa Polytechnic Institute in 1979. Then in 1984 I received a graduate degree in Industrial and Labor Relations at the University of Hawaii.
   I like my job very much but feel it is time to move to a higher position, one with greater challenges. I believe my experience and training make me prepared to do that. My present employer, in fact, is aware of my interest in this position and would be happy to write a letter of reference regarding my work.
   Although your advertisement stipulated no language requirement, I would like to mention that I am bilingual in Chinese and English, a fact which I believe would be helpful in working in a country such as Indonesia. I feel that this, plus my training and my eight years of experience, make me well-qualified to fill the position of Production Manager with your company.
   You may reach me by letter at the above address. I look forward to your reply.

6.6 *WRITING LETTERS BASED ON VISUAL INFORMATION*

Suggested procedure

1. Introduce the idea of letters of protest: Ask students what issues people might write letters of protest about and to whom they might write them. Students might suggest anything from a change in school policy to a proposed nuclear dump site.
2. Students read the instructions in part A. After students read the letter, they restate the writer's reasons for protesting the expansion as planned and show the writer's alternate suggestion by pointing to the appropriate spots on the map. Make sure students notice how the letter is organized: Paragraph 1 gives his purpose for writing; paragraphs 2, 3, 4, and 5 state his reasons; paragraph 6 gives his alternative suggestions; and paragraph 7 closes the letter.
3. Students read the instructions for part B and relate the task to the diagram. In small groups, students discuss what the letter should contain and how it should be

organized. Students write the letter individually, in class or for homework.
4. Students share their letters, comparing reasons and alternative suggestions, as well as organization and tone.

Sample letter
Dear Board of Education:

On behalf of the residents of the townhouses located on Franklin Street near the proposed college along River Road, I want to protest the building of this college as it is presently planned. We oppose it because:

First, the college will block our view of the river. This is disturbing not only for aesthetic reasons; it will also decrease the value of our houses if we are ever to sell them.

Second, there are two high-rise apartment buildings to the south of us blocking sunlight from that direction during a good part of the day. If the college is built to the west of us, that will decrease the amount of sunlight we get even more.

Third, parking will become an even bigger problem than it already is. From what we understand, there are no provisions for parking for college staff and students. This will only compound a problem that is already a serious one for this neighborhood, lack of space for on-street parking.

Fourth, the proposed main entrance to the college is on Franklin Street, which is a very narrow street already overloaded with street traffic. Having the college entrance on this street will cause an increase in traffic and unnecessary dangers to the residents of both the townhouses and the high-rise apartment buildings, many of whom are children.

If we have to accept the college being built in this location, we would like to suggest several changes in the plans. First, the college should create a parking area for college personnel, perhaps in the empty space on Chambers Street and West Street, so that our parking problems will not be increased. Second, the main entrance should be moved to either River Road or Chambers Street, thus relieving the amount of traffic on a residential street. Finally, the Board of Education should contribute to expanding and improving the park on River Road so that residents of the area have a pleasant and safe place to enjoy the view and the sunlight.

Thank you for your attention.

Sincerely,
(name)

6.7 PUNCTUATING: COLONS, SEMICOLONS, AND COMMAS

Suggested procedure

1. Students read the first set of instructions and discuss, in groups, sentences 1–3. They should discover that the colons in these sentences have two uses: (1) to explain further what was said already; what follows the colon is equal to one or more words before the colon (sentences 1 and 2); and (2) to punctuate the salutation in a business letter (sentence 3).
2. Students, in groups, read the next set of instructions and discuss the use of the semicolon. They should discover that a semicolon can be replaced with a period, but not with a comma. A semicolon is used: (1) to replace a period when two sentences are closely related (sentences 4 and 5); and (2) to separate items in a list if commas are used for other reasons (sentence 6).
3. Students read the letter to Mr. Ahmed in part B; they restate the purpose of the letter and the main points made. They then work in pairs on the task, putting in

suitable punctuation and capitalization. This task demands that they also decide where sentences begin and end. It is best if students read the letter aloud looking for sentence boundaries first. Then they can go back and decide on other punctuation. They will need to discuss alternatives, such as when to use a period and when to use a semicolon. Be sure students understand that there may be more than one way to punctuate this letter.

4. Students compare their letters. Alternatives can be shown on the board or on an overhead projector.

Sample letter

Dear Mr. Ahmed:

We are proud to announce the formation of a new and innovative international advertising agency, (:) Business Promoters International. We are convinced that you will recognize our potential as an extremely effective international advertising agency; (.) we are equally convinced that you will want to choose Business Promoters International to plan your international advertising campaigns.

Let us tell you a little about our personnel. Our five promoters together represent approximately 45 years of advertising experience throughout the world: the Far East, Europe, the Middle East, Latin America, and the United States. Their language and cultural backgrounds are as varied: Spanish, French, Chinese, Arabic, and Greek. Of course, all speak and write English fluently. This multilingual aspect of Business Promoters International is a great plus when handling the delicate matter of translating advertising slogans from one language to another. To illustrate the importance of this, you need only recall the unfortunate translation of the Pepsi slogan, "Come alive with Pepsi," which was translated in Taiwanese as, "Pepsi brings your ancestors back from the grave."

Business Promoters International is committed to designing advertising tailored to your company's marketing needs. We believe in what our name represents: (,) promoting your business throughout the world. We look forward to the opportunity of working with you.

Sincerely yours,
Brenda Kostas

6.8 PRACTICING WRITING BUSINESS LETTERS AND MEMOS

Suggested procedure

1. Students read through the list of topics and decide on one. Two students might want to work together on one of the memos or letters. (If your students are working in a business, an alternative topic for them could be a real issue that demands a memo or letter.)
2. Students who have chosen the same topic can talk for a few minutes about their ideas before writing. Writing should be done individually, however, either in class or for homework.
3. Students share their finished memos and letters in small groups first, where suggestions for revision can be made, and finally, with the whole class.

7 Stating an opinion I

Chapters 7 and 8 concern writing opinion or argumentative essays. Many students have to learn to write this kind of essay in order to pass certain writing proficiency tests in their schools or English courses; these students will find these two chapters particularly useful. However, the activities in the chapters can be useful for any student learning English. The skills are general and have application to any kind of writing.

7.1 ORGANIZING IDEAS

Suggested procedure

1. Introduce the activity by putting the word *lottery* on the board. Ask students what it means (a contest in which tickets are sold and winners are determined by a drawing) and how they feel about people playing a lottery.
2. Have students read the sentences. Ask someone to retell, in general, what the sentences say. What is the writer's opinion about the lottery? Why does the person feel this way?
3. Students work in groups rearranging the sentences. Be sure students pay attention to the underlined words and phrases. They should also decide how many paragraphs the essay will have and where each paragraph starts.
4. Groups compare their answers, explaining their reasons to one another.
5. Students should notice how the essay is organized: introduction stating opinion; first reason followed by an example; second reason followed by a detail; third reason followed by an example; and concluding paragraph, which restates the writer's opinion.

Answer

(d) I would like to express my concern at the growing number of lottery games in this country. (h) There are several reasons why I object to this kind of gambling.

(order) (j) First, the people who run the lotteries are taking substantial amounts of money away from people, many of whom are old and can least afford to lose it. (a) The elderly couple down the street from me, for example, spent over $20 on lottery tickets last week, and they have only their meager social security checks to support them.

(order) (f) Second, while I do not object to gambling in principle, I feel that this particular kind, where no skill is required on the part of the player, is especially offensive and deadening to the intellect. (c) People who want to gamble would be better off in places like Las Vegas or Hong Kong where they would at least be using some skill.

(order) (i) Finally, the places where lottery tickets are sold often attract undesirable people to otherwise quiet neighborhoods. (e) Just last month, a gang of youths tried to hassle people lined up to buy lottery tickets at my local newsstand, making a tremendous amount of noise in the attempt.

(order) (g) In conclusion, let me say that I do not wish to appear old-fashioned or anti-pleasure. (b) I only wish to express my opinion, namely, that lottery games of all types should be abolished.

7.2   *RELATING IDEAS: LINKING WORDS AND PHRASES*

Suggested procedure

1. Introduce the activity by asking students what is meant by the term *an ethnic community* (a community of people of the same language or race or culture or nationality). Ask students their opinions of living in a small ethnic community in a large, diverse country such as the United States. What would the advantages be? the disadvantages?
2. Students read the essay and restate the writer's main point and reasons for holding this opinion.
3. Students work in groups selecting the best words to fill the blanks for numbers 1–9. When finished, they should compare their answers with another group's answers.
4. In groups, students decide on words to fill the rest of the blanks. There may be several suggested for each; a group should come to agreement on one choice for each blank. The discussion for these decisions will be valuable for the students.
5. Students compare answers, explaining their choices.

> **Answers**
> 1. c) but (to show contrast; *on the contrary* would also show contrast, but a coordinating conjunction is needed, not a transition phrase, because of the comma)
> 2. a) at first (to show first in time, not first in order of the writer's points)
> 3. c) because (To show a reason for the writer's happiness. *Because of* is incorrect because the *of* demands a noun phrase following it; in this case, a noun clause follows.)
> 4. b) besides (to add another reason for the happiness)
> 5. d) for instance (to give an example of the kind of help received)
> 6. d) since (meaning: because; it gives the writer's reason for saying it was nice)
> 7. a) however (to show contrast; *but* also shows contrast, but could not be used in this position in the sentence)
> 8. c) when (the only word that fits the meaning)
> 9. c) and (adding a point)
> 10. but (To show contrast; coordinating conjunction needed. *However* is incorrect because of the punctuation; it would be preceded by a semicolon or period and followed by a comma.)
> 11. finally / eventually / gradually
> 12. on the contrary / in contrast / instead
> 13. and / so (coordinating conjunction needed)
> 14. yet / but (*However* is incorrect because of the punctuation; see item 10 above.)
> 15. because / since
> 16. like / including / such as (*For instance* or *for example* might work, but usually these are set off by commas.)
>
> *Note:* Students may come up with other acceptable answers for 10–16. Use your judgment.

6. Students should notice how this essay is developed. In paragraph 1, the writer states an opinion, in general terms. Paragraphs 2 and 3 describe the writer's experience. Paragraph 4 restates the writer's opinion, relating the personal experience to the opinion stated in paragraph 1. If students did 7.1, they can compare these two different ways of developing an opinion essay.

7.3   *SHOWING ATTITUDE*

Suggested procedure

1. Introduce the topic. Write this question on the board: Should laws restrict where people can smoke? Have students restate the question in a different way to check their comprehension of the meaning of the question. Let students answer the question, giving their opinions and reasons.
2. Students read the instructions and reply 1. Students may need to be reminded that they cannot do the exercise – choosing attitude words – until they have read the whole essay to find out the writer's opinion. Have one student restate the writer's opinion and reasons.
3. Students work in groups selecting the best words to fill the blanks.
4. Students compare their answers.

> **Answers to reply 1**
> 1. b) certainly (shows the writer's firmness of opinion)
> 2. a) in fact (adding more to the opinion; revealing more)
> 3. c) clearly (meaning: definitely)
> 4. c) unjustly (The writer thinks it's unfair for nonsmokers to have to pay for the bad consequences of smoking.)
> 5. c) unfortunately (The writer thinks it's unfortunate that smokers won't be considerate of others on their own.)
> 6. b) in my opinion (restating opinion)

5. Have students read reply 2. Ask someone to restate the writer's opinion and reasons. Does this writer agree with the first person?
6. Students work in groups selecting attitude words to fill the blanks. They should then compare their answers with others.

> **Answers to reply 2**
> 7. a) definitely (to show writer's certainty)
> 8. c) as far as I'm concerned (meaning: in my opinion)
> 9. d) as a matter of fact (meaning: in fact; this gives further evidence)
> 10. a) I believe (meaning: in my opinion)
> 11. a) naturally (meaning: of course)
> 12. a) clearly (to show writer's certainty)
> 13. d) in my opinion (restating writer's opinion)

7. Students write an essay on the same topic, either alone or with another student. If they wish, they can begin with one of the answers given, or they can use some of the ideas expressed in the replies and expand on them. This can be done in class or for homework.
8. Students read their essays to their small groups, getting comments and suggestions from the group members. They can then revise their essays if they wish. Revisions can be done for homework.
9. Students share their essays with the class.

7.4   *COMPARING TEXTS: FIRST PARAGRAPHS*

Suggested procedure

1. Introduce the topic by asking students to state some advantages to living in a large city. Students should then read the instructions for part A and the two paragraphs.
2. Students, in groups, decide on the better organized paragraph, giving reasons for their decision.

> **Answer**
> CHOICE 2. Choice 1 *seems* to group reasons together *(In the first place, Second)*, but when analyzed, the groupings prove to be faulty. For one thing, both the first and second groups have to do with education. Also, although there are four reasons given, the transition word *finally* is used for the third reason, while *moreover* is used for the last reason.
>   Choice 2 discusses each reason in a category: 1) education, 2) culture and recreation, 3) jobs. Details are given about each. Also, transition words are used correctly.

3. Students read the instructions for part B. Small groups can decide if they want to follow one of the suggestions given for getting ideas: brainstorming or free-writing.
4. Encourage students to make an outline or a partial outline before starting to write their paragraph.
5. Students share their first paragraphs with others and the class.

> **Sample first paragraph**
>   There are definite advantages to living in a rural area or small town. For one thing, the quality of life is better. The pace of life is slower than you find in a busy, rushing city, and with fewer people, there is less crowding. Second, it is healthier to live in a rural area. There are fewer industries, so there is less pollution than in a city. Finally, there is more of a feeling of community in a rural area or small town. You know your neighbors, and you talk to them, which is something that does not happen often in a big city. Let us look at each of these points in more detail.

6. Students may wish to write a whole essay on this topic using the paragraph they wrote or choice 2 in part A as their first paragraph. They will need to develop each point in more detail in the body of the essay as well as add a concluding paragraph. This can be done for homework. Results should be shared with the class.

7.5   *WRITING AN ESSAY BASED ON A CONVERSATION*

Suggested procedure

1. Introduce the topic by putting the word *farming* on the board and asking students to suggest words they associate with it. Ask them to explain each word they give. Then have students compare farming as they know it in their country and farming in the United States. Are things done differently? What is similar?
2. Students read the instructions and restate the various tasks called for. So that the

tasks will not seem overwhelming to students, reassure them that they will work in stages.

3. Two students read the conversation aloud. Ask students to underline or jot down words they don't know as they listen. Have students restate what they understood from the conversation. Then go over vocabulary that students ask for. Some words may be:

> *productivity:* the amount of crops the land can produce
> *topsoil:* the surface (or topmost) layer of soil
> *tree belts:* trees planted in rows to protect soil from winds
> *erosion:* the wearing away of topsoil by water or wind
> *irrigating:* supplying dry land with water by pumping water from streams through ditches
> *fertilizers:* natural substances or man-made chemicals which cause greater growth
> *pesticides:* chemicals used to kill insects
> *contaminate:* to make impure; to poison

4. Have students reread the conversation silently. Then ask students to restate the issue the farmers are discussing – the question of whether U.S. farmers can continue to farm the way they are farming now and still have good soil and make money. Ask students which farmer they side with, A or B. They should choose one point of view.
5. Students with similar points of view work in small groups first writing one sentence which clearly states their opinion, and then making an outline of ideas they can include in their essay to support that opinion.
6. Students write their essay. They should keep in mind that this essay will be an editorial in a newspaper; it should be convincing to readers and should use a more formal tone than the conversation does.
7. Students read their first drafts to their group and give one another suggestions for improvement.
8. Students write their second drafts. These can be done as homework. Final drafts should be shared with the class.

Sample essay

American farmers are producing 13% of the world's wheat, 25% of its corn, and 62% of its soybeans. They have been labeled "miracle farmers" because of this tremendous productivity, and they deserve it. Farming has become a big money-making business, and that's the way it should stay.

There are those who protest some farming practices, who say that topsoil is being destroyed or that water is being used up. They suggest farmers do things like quit irrigating, farm less land, plant tree belts, or terrace. If they want to stay in business as farmers, they cannot do that and survive. Tree belts and terraces interfere with machinery and slow down the work they do. Without irrigating, most of the land would be worthless as farm land. Yields would go down, and profits would suffer.

Farmers have always believed that the bigger they farm, the better off they'll be. The more crops they can plant and harvest and sell, the more money they'll make. I also believe that. Nobody can convince me that farming less land is efficient.

People also protest using pesticides and chemical fertilizers. Farmers have to do that to take care of the insects and weeds that would otherwise attack crops. More weeds and insects mean lower productivity, and consequently, lower prices.

I do agree that we need to worry about saving soil and water for future generations, but I believe it's not farmers' responsibility alone. The government and agricultural experts have to share that responsibility, too. Meanwhile, farmers have to be concerned about making a living for themselves and their families. Productivity and profits are still the farmer's primary concern.

(Note: This essay was written *about* farmers. Students could also use the first person, writing as though a farmer wrote the editorial.)

7.6   *WRITING AN ESSAY BASED ON VISUAL INFORMATION*

Suggested procedure

In groups, students look at the drawings and talk about what issues the drawings suggest to them. They should select one drawing to focus on, state the issue, and give their opinions on the issue and reasons for those opinions. Then individuals write their essay. An *issue* is a concern or problem that is shared by many people. The issues are:

a) Cars are parked in front of a hospital emergency entrance, thus blocking the entrance for incoming ambulances and violating signs prohibiting parking.
b) People have piled garbage on the sidewalk or street, ignoring the sign that asks them to keep the streets clean.
c) One sign indicates that the parks are for people to enjoy; yet another sign forbids people from walking on the grass. This seems to be a mixed message.
d) "Beautiful" Springdale suffers from air pollution.

7.7   *ADDING EXAMPLES AND DETAILS*

Suggested procedure

1. Introduce the topic by asking students how older people are treated in their countries. What is people's attitude toward older people? What happens to a person when he or she gets old? Ask how they think older people *should* be treated.
2. Students read and restate the instructions, then read the paragraph about older people. In groups, students decide what the writer's main point is and write that main point or proposition *using their own words* in the blank provided. They do the same with the two reasons given. They then compare their answers.

> **Sample answer:**
> WRITER'S MAIN POINT: Society should value and appreciate older people instead of ignoring them.
> REASON 1: Older people feel unappreciated and unwanted when they are ignored.
> REASON 2: Older people can contribute a lot in knowledge and experience to society and to their families.

3. Students, in groups, brainstorm examples and details to explain each of the two reasons. Encourage students to use specific examples (people they know) and/or specific details. Each group should develop a list of ideas for each reason, which individuals can choose from when they write their expanded essay.
4. Each student writes the expanded essay. They may want to delete the statement of

reasons from paragraph 1 and make each reason the topic (first) sentence of paragraphs 2 and 3. (Thus, paragraph 2 is about how older people can feel unwanted and unloved, and paragraph 3 is about what older people can contribute to society.) Another alternative is to leave the first paragraph as it is, and restate each reason *using different words* in paragraphs 2 and 3.

5. After completing paragraphs 2 and 3, students share their writing and discuss what could be said in the last or concluding paragraph. They then write their last paragraph.

6. Students read one another's essays, looking at such things as strength of detail or example, and whether the essay is convincing to a reader.

Sample list or outline:
1. Reason 1: If ignored, older people feel unwanted and unloved.
   a) example: my mother's friend Emily in a nursing home – depressed, sad
   b) example: my neighbor living alone, not visited by his children, lonely, deteriorating
2. Reason 2: Older people can contribute to family and society
   a) if they live with or are close to children and grandchildren, family can learn from them, such as what life was like years ago or certain skills (for example, bread baking or carpentry)
   b) society can learn about the past, sense of history

Essay
[First paragraph as is]
We only need to look at the older people we see living alone in our neighborhoods or in nearby nursing homes to know how these people are affected by their families not paying attention to them. My mother's friend, Emily, for example, is in a nursing home far away from all of her children.She is sad and depressed and is having a hard time recovering from the stroke she had several months ago. Another example is my neighbor who lives all alone and whose children rarely visit him. He, too, is lonely and, in fact, his health is rapidly deteriorating, mostly because of his emotional state. Surely we owe older people better treatment than this.

Instead of ignoring older people, we should welcome them in our families and society. They are rich in knowledge and experience. Their grandchildren can learn much from them – from what life was like in the past to skills like bread baking and carpentry. Society, too, can benefit from their knowledge of the past, thus gaining a deeper sense of history and perhaps even benefiting from their mistakes.

It's time for us to take a look at what we are doing to older people in this society. We must learn to value what older people have done for us and can still do for us. We must change both our attitudes and our actions. After all, we will be in their shoes someday and will certainly want respect and love from those around us.

7.8 DEBATING ISSUES

Suggested procedure

1. Introduce the topic. Write this question on the board: Are computers good educators? Ask students for their opinions and reasons or explanations.

2. Tell students they will read a newspaper article and guest interviews on this issue. Students read the one-paragraph article and restate what the two sides of the issue are.

3. Read the interview question: Should computers be encouraged in schools? Ask students to predict what some reasons might be to encourage computers in schools and what some reasons might be to discourage computers in schools. Students, in groups, read the six replies to the interview question. Groups should restate what each of the replies says.

4. Tell students to choose one side of the issue (whether or not computers are good educators and should be encouraged in schools) and write an editorial on the issue. Students should read the steps suggested in the instructions. They may follow these steps if they wish.

   For classes where more help is needed, you might elicit from students reasons for and against the issue. These can be listed on the board in two columns: 1) For computers in schools; 2) Against computers in schools. Then students can choose from one or the other list when writing their essay.

5. Students share their completed essays, giving one another suggestions for improvement in such areas as organization, clarity, supporting details and examples, effective beginning, effective ending, and persuasiveness. They should be given opportunity to revise if they wish, perhaps for homework.

Sample essay

Computers are becoming more and more common in our schools. While children may be temporarily fascinated by computers, their parents and teachers should realize that these machines as used in schools today are detrimental to their education and their general well-being.

If you examine the kinds of activities most "educational" computer programs ask children to do today, you will find primarily two kinds: games and drills. While I do not object to children playing games on computers, I believe school is not the proper place for game-playing. Computer games can be played at home or in video arcades. As far as drill exercises are concerned, they are not the best way to learn. Children can learn much more from, for example, the challenges of problem solving where some creativity and imagination are required. Until we get more sophisticated computer programs for real learning, let's leave computers out of our schools.

Letting children use computers during school hours only encourages them to be inactive and unsociable at a time in their life when they need to be active and to learn how to get along with others. I know a seven-year-old, for example, who is hooked on computers. She spends all of her free time during and after school using a computer, mainly for playing games. She is pale and unhealthy looking from spending so much time indoors, and, worse yet, she has no friends. She needs to be playing actively outdoors, not inside with only a computer as a companion.

We need to evaluate what is going on in our schools regarding computers. Computers may be a wonderful aid to learning in the future, but at the moment, they are harmful to our children. We need to think much more carefully before we hop onto the computer bandwagon.

7.9   *PUNCTUATING: WHEN AND WHEN NOT TO*

Suggested procedure

1. Students, in groups, read sentences 1–5 in part A and discuss the use of or lack of punctuation. After a few minutes, ask them to state the reasons for each punctuation

mark used. (Students may want to review what they learned about punctuation in previous chapters, especially in exercises 2.7 and 3.9.)

> Sentences 1b and 2b need quotation marks because the exact words of the speakers are quoted. A comma follows a reporting word (*say, ask*) when there is a direct quotation (sentences 1b and 2b), but not when there is an indirect one (sentences 1a and 2a).
>
> Sentence 3a: The dependent clause comes at the end of the sentence, so no comma is needed.
>
> Sentence 3b: A dependent clause begins the sentence, so a comma is needed.
>
> Sentences 5a, b, c: The transition word *therefore* is set off by commas no matter where it appears in the sentence. In 5c, the dependent clause comes before the independent clause, so a comma is needed.

2. In groups, students edit the essay in part B. They will have to correct wrong use of commas, periods, and quotation marks as well as wrong use of capital letters (see exercise 1.8).

Answer

Poor People and Nutrition

[All words in a title are capitalized except "small" words, such as prepositions and conjunctions.]

Nutrition is for people who have the power to buy any kind of food they want. Food is at their doorstep, and if they do not have the money, the government protects and feeds them. These people can afford to take care of their bodies and their appearance through good nutrition.

However, in my country(,) diet and nutrition are not popular subjects. You cannot talk about proper diet and nutrition to most people here because the words have no meaning for the masses. Only a tiny group of privileged people can afford to understand these words.

People live from day to day. They eat whatever they can get in any day. Sometimes they have one meal a day, and they wake up the next day with nothing to eat. There is a lack of everything, and there is no money to buy anything.

We are not protected by the government. We eat only what we can provide for ourselves, and most of us have no money. Therefore, when a doctor says, "Watch your diet and think about nutrition," the words are empty. They have no meaning. We eat what we have for each day. We cannot afford nutrition.

7.10   *PRACTICING WRITING OPINION ESSAYS*

Suggested procedure

1. Students read through the topics and pick one to write on. You might give students a day or two to think about the topics before deciding on one.
2. Once they have picked a topic, encourage students to use some of the techniques they have used in this chapter for getting and organizing ideas: free-writing (see 7.4 in Student's Book), brainstorming (7.4 in Student's Book), listing or outlining (7.5, 7.7 in Student's Book).
3. Students write first drafts, either for homework or in class. If they write in class, it gives you an opportunity to move around helping students clarify their ideas by asking questions. You can also see who gets stuck and try to find out why.

4. Students get feedback on first drafts and revise.
5. Students share revised essays, getting feedback on clarity and logic, and form (paragraphing, punctuation, spelling, correctness), and on style (is it convincing?).

8 Stating an opinion II

8.1 ORGANIZING IDEAS

Suggested procedure

1. Introduce the topic by putting this quotation on the board or on an overhead projector: "A woman's place is in the home." Ask students what it means and what they think of it.
2. Students read through the sentences to find out what the writer's opinion is. Ask them to restate the opinion.
3. In groups, students put sentences in logical order and divide the essay into paragraphs.
4. Students compare their results, explaining the relationships between sentences.

Answer

(c) You often hear people say, "A woman's place is in the home." (k) Many traditionalists support this statement, saying that a woman's first responsibility is to her husband and children. (g) Others, however, find this notion old-fashioned in today's world of tight budgets and good child-care facilities. (e) I am one of those who believe that mothers are not neglecting their responsibilities by working outside the home. (b) In fact, I believe that children benefit when their mothers work.

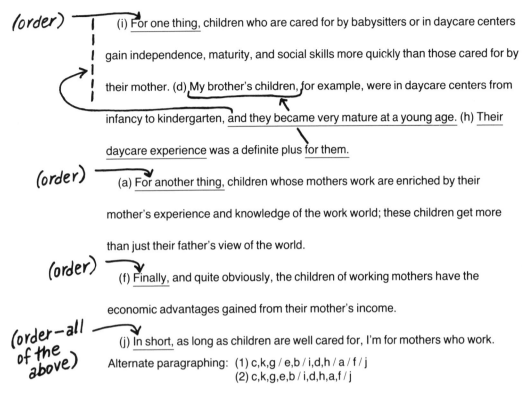

(order)   (i) For one thing, children who are cared for by babysitters or in daycare centers gain independence, maturity, and social skills more quickly than those cared for by their mother. (d) My brother's children, for example, were in daycare centers from infancy to kindergarten, and they became very mature at a young age. (h) Their daycare experience was a definite plus for them.

(order)   (a) For another thing, children whose mothers work are enriched by their mother's experience and knowledge of the work world; these children get more than just their father's view of the world.

(order)   (f) Finally, and quite obviously, the children of working mothers have the economic advantages gained from their mother's income.

(order – all of the above)   (j) In short, as long as children are well cared for, I'm for mothers who work.

Alternate paragraphing: (1) c,k,g / e,b / i,d,h / a / f / j
(2) c,k,g,e,b / i,d,h,a,f / j

5. Ask students to analyze how the essay is organized: Paragraph 1 starts with a popular quotation and describes two opposite opinions about the idea. It goes on to state the writer's opinion (writer's proposition or thesis or opinion statement – sentences e and b). Paragraphs 2, 3, and 4 discuss three reasons that support (prove) this opinion; paragraph 5 concludes by restating the writer's opinion.

8.2   *RELATING IDEAS: LINKING WORDS AND PHRASES*

Suggested procedure

1. Introduce the topic by asking students what places in the world suffer from hunger. What are some of the causes of hunger in these places?
2. Students silently skim (read very quickly) the essay on hunger in Africa. After this quick reading, have students jot down words they remember from the reading and then share their list of words in small groups and/or with the class. Ask: What is the writer's opinion about the main cause of hunger? What can be done about it?
3. Students read the essay again, this time more slowly. Ask students if there are any words they don't understand. Some new words may include:

> *drought*: a long period with no rain
> *famine:* a serious shortage of food
> *poverty:* the condition of being poor

4. Students, if they have not done so already, state the writer's main point (the cause of hunger in Africa is poverty, not drought and overpopulation) and what the writer thinks must be done about poverty (change farming practices so that African farmers can earn a decent living and decrease the size of their families).
5. Students, in groups, choose linking words for numbers 1–12. For 13–18, they fill in the blanks with a word or phrase that makes sense to the group.
6. Groups compare answers. Students should notice that more than one choice is possible for 13–18.

Answers
1. d) such as   2. a) also   3. b) such as   4. d) however   5. c) and
6. a) on the contrary (to show contrast to the previous idea)   7. b) first
8. c) but   9. a) then   10. b) consequently (meaning: as a result)
11. b) and   12. a) but
13. Next / Now / Second   14. namely / that is   15. However / Nevertheless
16. Therefore / Thus   17. In conclusion / To conclude / Finally / Therefore
18. namely / that is

NOTE: Other words may be possible; you will have to use your judgment.

7. Ask students to analyze the organization of this essay: Paragraph 1 defines a popular explanation for hunger in Africa; paragraph 2 admits these problems, but negates them as the real causes and gives the writer's opinion about the real cause of hunger (the writer's proposition or thesis or opinion statement). Paragraph 3 explains the writer's plan for the essay, to discuss each problem one by one. Paragraph 4 discusses problem 1 and suggests a long-term solution. Paragraph 5 discusses problem 2 and suggests a long-term solution. Paragraph 6 restates the writer's thesis (the real cause of hunger is poverty) and urges readers to recall this when hearing about Africa's hunger in the future. Students may want to compare the organization of this essay with that of essay 8.1.

8.3   SHOWING ATTITUDE

Suggested procedure

1. Introduce the topic by asking students if they think watching violence on TV affects people in any way.
2. Students read instructions and reply 1. Have one student restate this person's opinion. Then students, in small groups, choose attitude words to fill the blanks. When finished, groups compare answers.

Answers to reply 1:
1. b) undoubtedly (meaning: without a doubt; certainly)
2. a) certainly (meaning: definitely)
3. d) of course (meaning: naturally)
4. c) in fact (meaning: as a matter of fact)
5. b) frankly (meaning: to be honest)
6. a) in my opinion
7. d) definitely

3. Students read reply 2, restate the person's opinion, and choose attitude words for 8–13. They then compare results.

> **Answers to reply 2:**
> 8. b) as far as I'm concerned (meaning: in my opinion)
> 9. a) certainly (meaning: without a doubt)
> 10. c) as a matter of fact (meaning: in fact)
> 11. a) personally
> 12. c) in my opinion
> 13. b) in short

4. Students, working either alone or with a group, write a complete essay on the topic taking one side or the other. If students choose to write alone, they may wish to talk over some arguments for their point of view before beginning to write. Encourage students to use personal examples, if applicable, or support from what they have read or know about from others.
5. Students read each other's essays when they are finished, getting feedback from one another on content and style. They can revise their essays for homework.

8.4 *WRITING FIRST AND LAST PARAGRAPHS*

Suggested procedure

1. Students analyze the last paragraphs of the essays mentioned in the instructions to part A. (It will make students' work easier if the last paragraphs are put onto a transparency and shown on an overhead projector. Students can focus more easily than if they have to shuffle through their books looking for each of the relevant paragraphs.) They should notice:

> 7.1: The writer shows concern about how readers may judge him/her and restates his/her reason or purpose for writing the essay (to express concern about a situation).
> 7.2: The writer admits the advantage of living in an ethnic community, but highlights the major disadvantage (not learning enough about the new culture). The writer puts this realization into a meaningful context, that of a valuable lesson learned.
> 8.1: The writer summarizes the main point in one final, to-the-point, sentence.
> 8.2: The writer restates the main point of the essay, asking readers to remember that point when hearing about the topic again. In a sense, the writer is also reminding readers of the importance of this topic, implying that the words *drought, overpopulation,* and *famine* are words – and issues – we hear about frequently.

Students should become aware that just restating the main point of an essay in the final paragraph is often not enough to convince readers that this is an important issue and that readers should believe or even agree with the writer. Putting the issue into a larger, more global context is one way of making the issue itself meaningful. It is a way of giving readers a reason to place importance on what the writer is saying. Another way of making an issue meaningful and thus important is what the writer in 8.2 did, reminding readers that this is an issue often heard or read about.

2. Students read the essay in part A. Have several students restate the writer's proposition and support for the proposition. In groups, students discuss what could be included in a final paragraph, keeping in mind that the purpose of the essay is to convince someone of their opinion.

3. Students write a final paragraph, either in a group or individually, and share their results.

> **Sample last paragraph**
> In order to alleviate these serious problems of traffic congestion, parking, and air and noise pollution in our large cities, we should ban cars from entering these cities on weekdays. This is one workable way to start solving some of the ever-increasing problems faced by our modern cities. We must work now to create livable cities for tomorrow.

4. Students analyze the first paragraphs of the essays mentioned in the instructions for part B. (Again, if possible, use the overhead projector.)

> 7.1: Sentence 1 states the writer's opinion: concern about lottery games. Sentence 2 mentions that the writer has reasons for this opinion (but does not state the reasons). Sentence 2 serves as a transition to the rest of the essay; it forces readers to ask: What are the reasons? Readers expect the rest of the essay to answer this question.
>
> 7.2: Sentence 1 gives the writer's proposition (thesis or opinion statement). Sentence 2 structures the rest of the essay: The proposition will be explained through personal example.
>
> 8.1: The essay begins with a well-known quotation. Sentence 2 tells why many people support this notion. Sentence 3 tells why many people oppose the notion. Sentence 4 states the writer's opinion (opposing the idea suggested by the quotation), and sentence 5 goes even further than merely opposing the quotation (by asserting that children benefit when mothers work).
>
> 8.2: Paragraph 1 states a problem and two popular notions of their causes. Paragraph 2 admits that these two causes increase the problem, but asserts that there is a deeper cause for the problem (poverty). The writer's thesis statement comes in sentence 3 of this second paragraph.
>
> 8.4.A: Sentence 1 states a problem; sentence 2 describes a solution (the writer's opinion or proposition).

Students should see some of the ways opinion essays can begin: describe a problem or situation; quote someone and discuss the quotation; state a personal concern; mention an issue and state your opinion about it. They should also see that the writer's thesis or opinion statement very often comes toward the end of the first paragraph (and can even come in the second paragraph, as in 8.2). In several cases, the last sentence of paragraph 1 structures the rest of the essay by telling the reader how the point of view will be supported.

5. Students read the essay in part B. In groups, they state what point of view (opinion) is expressed and what is said to support or develop that point of view. Groups discuss what the first paragraph should contain and how it might begin and end.

6. Students write their first paragraphs, either alone or in pairs. They share their first paragraph.

Sample first paragraph

Do you ever feel dissatisfied with your job? Do you have a desire to search for more exciting, more challenging work? If you've answered "yes" to both of those questions, think carefully before you act. In my opinion, it is generally not a good idea to quit a secure job in order to find something "more fulfilling." Having a sure job today, I feel, is much more important than searching for the perfect job. Let me explain.

7. As a way of briefly reviewing the features of last paragraphs, you might have students analyze the final paragraph of this essay, 8.4B. They should see that the writer restates the main point and puts the issue of the essay – job security – into a larger, more meaningful context – that of personal security.

Note: This exercise can be time-consuming if done carefully, especially the analyses of the first and last paragraphs, but you will find the work well worth students' time. You may want to divide the work into two lessons, however.

8.5   SELECTING AND ORDERING INFORMATION

Suggested procedure

1. Students read the instructions and then quickly read the first paragraph of the essay. After their quick reading, ask students to give you words they noted as they read; write the words on the board and check to see if students understand all the words. These terms may need explanation:

> *aggressive competitive sports:* sports that are very physical, with a lot of bodily contact, seeming to be almost hostile (examples: ice hockey, soccer)
> *aggression:* hostile action or behavior; acting like others are enemies
> *brutality:* the quality of being harsh, violent

Ask: What is the topic? the issue? the writer's opinion? If students aren't sure, encourage them to guess and reassure them that they can find out by reading the passage again.
2. Students read the paragraph again (aloud or silently). They should notice that the writer's opinion is given in the last sentence of the paragraph.
3. In groups, students read aloud all the points listed under *Choose from these points.* They should restate each point in their own words (to make sure they understand vocabulary and meaning). As they read, each person checks off points to include in the rest of the essay. Students then discuss which points to delete and which to keep. Not everyone in each group needs to agree on exactly the same items, but students should be able to explain why they want to delete or include certain points.
4. Students group the points chosen into paragraphs.
5. Individuals write out the essay, adding necessary linking words, phrases, sentences, and adding a concluding paragraph if needed. Writing can be done in class or for homework.
6. Students share their results. There will be many different ways to complete the essay, depending on what the writer decides to emphasize.

Sample answer (underlined words are added)

[First paragraph]

<u>It is certainly true that</u> a person in a large crowd watching a sporting event feels anonymous in that crowd and therefore feels less inhibited about showing aggressive behavior when excited about something that happens on the playing field. Fans get more excited when watching rough sports like soccer, hockey, or boxing than they do when watching sports like golf, gymnastics, or swimming. <u>In fact,</u> I have often seen shouting matches and even fights among spectators at college soccer games. Young people especially tend to imitate sports heroes, and if they see those heroes punching one another in a boxing match, they may try to do the same.

<u>But it is not only fans who are affected by rough sports.</u> Research with high school and college athletes finds that students who participate in more aggressive sports like hockey or soccer show anger more quickly than those who participate in sports like swimming, where competitors do not come near each other.

<u>Many people believe that</u> social problems like unemployment and extreme nationalism may be major reasons for violence among sports fans. <u>Others say that</u> sometimes sports fans drink, and this can contribute to violence and rowdiness. <u>Both of these statements may be partially true, but they are not the whole truth.</u> <u>From my own experience and what I have read, I conclude that aggressive sports encourage aggression in both viewers and participants of these sports. Perhaps we should consider more carefully the harm that can result from what we call "sports."</u>

8.6   *COMPARING TEXTS*

Suggested procedure

1. Students read the instructions and restate them. Groups read essay 1 silently, then discuss what the issue is and what the writer's opinion is. They do the same for essay 2.
2. Groups talk about the two essays, focusing on relevance of ideas, connections between sentences, how ideas are grouped, and how the essays are paragraphed. They choose the best-written essay and explain their choice to other groups.

Answer
Essay 1 is better written than essay 2. Its point of view is clear in paragraph 1. Paragraphs 2 and 3 each stick to one point. Sentences follow one another logically, developing ideas further with each new sentence. Although essay 2's point of view can be understood in paragraph 1, the paragraph is quite disorganized. Sentences do not seem to follow one another with any logic. The same is true for paragraphs 2, 3, 4, and 5. For example, paragraph 3 introduces

the idea of health in sentence 1, but then jumps to money in sentence 2; sentence 3 goes back to health again, and sentence 4 to money once more. Sentence 5 talks about enjoyment. Other paragraphs are just as illogical.

3. Students, after discussing the faults of essay 2, should have a fairly good idea of how to improve the essay. The major problem is its organization, so they will want to talk about how to group ideas in a better, more logical way. Encourage groups to make an outline or a list of points they want to make in the order they want to make them before they begin to write.
4. Students rewrite essay 2. They may add or change sentences if they wish. They compare their essays when they finish.

Sample of rewritten essay
No More Video Games

Teenagers are spending far too much time and money in video arcades these days. Video games should be done away with. They are nothing but a waste of time, money, and energy. Teenagers should be doing valuable things like reading, studying, and going to concerts and museums.

Young people could spend their time in far healthier places than inside video arcades. The lights are often dim and the games are noisy, which damages people's eyes and ears. Doing physical activities in the open air would be much healthier for teenagers. I am sure they would enjoy it more, too.

A lot of money is spent by teenagers on these games. They think nothing of spending ten or twenty dollars in an afternoon or evening just to have the satisfaction of sometimes beating an electronic machine.

These games are nothing but a waste of people's time. Playing video games does not allow people to use any of their natural creativity. There is also no opportunity for physical exercise, something young people are sadly lacking these days.

Video arcades should be banned from our cities and towns. Teenagers would be much better off without the temptation these places provide.

8.7   ADDING EXAMPLES AND DETAILS

Suggested procedure

1. Introduce the topic by putting this phrase on the board: *cooperative buying*. Ask students to figure out what it means. If they can't do so, ask them to read the first paragraph of the essay and give the meaning. Ask if they have ever had experience with this kind of buying.
2. Students read the instructions and paragraph 2 of the essay. In groups, they should restate (in their own words) the writer's main point and the three reasons given to support the opinion.

Answer
MAIN POINT: People should buy cooperatively because of its advantages.
REASON 1: It's cheaper than buying something alone.
REASON 2: You have less worry with less to take care of.
REASON 3: You might develop good friendships.

3. Groups list examples and/or details to illustrate each reason. Individuals write out the essay, developing each reason into a separate paragraph, and adding a concluding paragraph. They share their results.

Sample expanded essay
[Paragraphs 1 and 2]
Buying a new piece of equipment like a car or computer or washing machine on your own is a large expense. Very likely, this is a machine you do not need to use every hour of every day. Economically, it makes sense to share the use of this machine, thereby also sharing the cost. Sharing a washing machine with one or two families, for example, can cut the cost for you in half or in thirds. Instead of paying $300 to buy the machine, you pay $150 or $100. That's a big savings.

You also have less to worry about if the machine breaks down. You are not only sharing the use of the machine; you are also sharing the responsibility for its upkeep. In other words, you're splitting the headaches two or even three ways.

There is an added advantage to buying cooperatively. You may make some close friends. It's hard to share the use and cost of a piece of equipment without getting to know your partners quite well. I've shared the ownership of a lawn mower for three years, and my partner and I have become fast friends because of it. In fact, we even help mow one another's lawns now.

To anyone considering buying an expensive piece of equipment, I suggest you consider cooperative buying. I promise a challenging, but rewarding, endeavor.

8.8   DEBATING ISSUES

Suggested procedure

1. Students read the instructions.
2. Read the question: Should those over 70 be forced to retire? Ask students their opinion. Then together read the introductory paragraph and interview question.
3. Assign 7 students to read the 7 replies to the question. Ask other students to restate what each one said.
4. Small groups discuss what side of the issue each person supports and why.
5. Either in pairs or individually, students write an editorial supporting one side of the issue. They can follow the steps suggested in the instructions or they can use their own method of organizing ideas and writing.
6. Students share their editorials when finished.

Sample essay
In my view, forcing people to retire at the age of 70 is criminal. It is not only unfair to the older person; it is also wasting a valuable resource. Let me explain my point of view.

My mother worked until she was 73, and then she retired because she chose to. She was a dependable and experienced worker, and she contributed a lot to her employer. Her employer and her fellow workers appreciated her staying on the job longer than she had to because her services were so valuable. In addition, she had a long period of time to train her replacement, for which both her boss and her successor were grateful. My mother is an example, I think, of an older person who was a service to her company even when she was older than 70.

Companies who insist on forcing older people to retire, I believe, are losing something of value. It's not only the companies who gain, however. The Social Security system or company pension plan, and therefore the economy, also gain, since these older people are putting even more money into the Social Security or pension system rather than drawing out retirement benefits. The longer people work, the less it costs somebody to pay for their retirement years.

Many people view older people as a detriment to the work force. I don't. I see them as vital contributors to their places of work as well as to society as a whole.

8.9   PUNCTUATING: WHEN AND WHEN NOT TO

Suggested procedure

1. Students read the instructions. Working in groups or pairs, they should correct punctuation, capitalization, and paragraphing. They share their results when finished, being sure to explain the reason for each change they make.

> **Answer**
> Dear Editor,(:)
>   I am writing this letter to complain about the Morrison County Highway Department neglecting to repair County Route 10 between the towns of Wadena and St. Cloud. Many cars have been seriously damaged by bumps in the road. In fact, people are even afraid to take Route 10 to St. Cloud for shopping because they fear for the welfare of their cars.
>   Unfortunately, there are more serious problems than cars. (;)(:) People's health has also been in danger. There have been several seriously ill patients, for example, who had to be moved from Riverview Hospital in Wadena to Franklin Memorial Hospital in St. Cloud. The condition of the Wadena–St. Cloud Road has forced ambulances to take a longer route through the town of Brainerd. This has been an inconvenience, an added expense, and, at times, even a danger for these patients. They ask such questions as these: Can't we do something about repairing Route 10 soon so we can return to our homes in the most direct and comfortable way? Do we have to wait for a serious accident before getting Route 10 repaired?
>   We *all* need this road repaired. Can't the Highway Department do it soon?
>   A Concerned Citizen of Wadena

2. Optional: In groups, students discuss the questions at the end of the exercise. If you have students of different cultural backgrounds, their answers to the questions might differ. The resulting discussion could be quite interesting. If they develop a list of topics (in answer to the last question), you might suggest they write a letter addressing one of the topics.

8.10   PRACTICING WRITING OPINION ESSAYS

Suggested procedure

1. Students read the topics and pick one to write on. You can suggest they use one of these strategies for getting and organizing ideas: free-writing (see 7.4 in Student's Book), brainstorming (7.4 in Student's Book), listing or outlining (7.5, 7.7 in Student's Book), or word association (similar to the activity described in 3.5, Teacher's Manual). An extension of word association is a technique called

"mapping," where the writer places words that are closely related next to one another on the page. This is an example of one person's "mapping" of topic (j), an environmental issue (acid rain):

West
Virginia

effect on
fish

acid rivers
+ lakes

smokestacks
sulphur
dioxide

Ohio
factories

winds

costs of
controls

acid rain

dying
trees

Black Forest (Germany)

New York
State

Canada

the Green
Party

N.Y./Vermont
governors protest

Canadian-U.S.
agreements

Students may choose to focus on only one or two parts of their "maps" when they write their essays, since writing about everything may be too big a job for one essay. The nice thing about the mapping technique is that some organizing is already done.

2. After spending 10 to 15 minutes getting and organizing ideas, students can begin to write, perhaps for 30 minutes. At this point, even though they are not finished, it might be a good idea for students to read what they have to a small group in order to get listeners' (readers) questions. Readers' questions are a very good way for writers to find out where they need to clarify or to say more, or where there is something illogical about the order in which they said things, and what else they need to say to complete the essay.

3. Students continue writing, perhaps for homework.

4. Students compare their finished essays. If time permits, after getting feedback from other students in their groups, they can revise their essays.

5. Final drafts should be shared with the class.